Praise for
Marketing in a World of Digital Sharing

"Sujata Ramnarayan's excellent book does several things that I have not seen in other treatments of this subject. She takes a reasoned perspective on a topic that is often full of hyperbole. The book is filled with advice for the marketer that is both practical and strategic. It helps the marketer to leverage social media where it can best impact business performance. I highly recommend the book."
- Gordon Wyner, Editor-In-Chief, Marketing Management

"This practical guide to social media marketing cuts through the noise with clear advice on how to turn strategy into practice. With the help of effective charts and analysis, the reader can gain real insight into social media's influence in corporate marketing. By showing how building quality content in social media is no longer an option for corporations, this is also a lesson in building a brand by listening to your customers. "
-Rajesh Subramaniam, SVP, Global Marketing and Customer Experience, FedEx Services

"Owned social media presence is critical to generating earned media, which is where the growing value and rewards come in for social media marketing. This important book will help you to understand these concepts and reality to better evaluate, plan, and execute your social media marketing efforts."
- Devin Redmond, CEO and Co-Founder, SocialiQ Networks

"Are you overwhelmed by the changing digital landscape? If so, Sujata's book is a must read with actionable insights, tips on digital sharing, and more."
-Porter Gale, Former VP of Marketing at Virgin America and author of "Your Network is Your Net Worth"

Marketing in a World of Digital Sharing

Are you drowning in social media noise and chaos?

Sujata Ramnarayan, Ph.D.

MP
MARS Publishing

Published by MARS Publishing.

Library of Congress Control Number: 2012913227

Printed in the United States of America

ISBN-13: 978-0-9859386-0-4 (Print)

ISBN-13: 978-0-9859386-1-1 (ebook)

Editing by Joanne Shwed

Acknowledgements

I owe my work to many too numerous to name. However, I would like to acknowledge a few that were invaluable. This work, of course, would not have been possible without the creative contribution of many other works cited in this book that aided in its creation. I would specially like to acknowledge Pew Internet for making its data available for re-use. My thanks also go to founders of companies that I have been advising – SocialiQ Networks and CitySocial. My conversations and interactions with them at different points helped me immensely in my thinking when writing this book.

My work with CareerCloset and the Silicon Valley American Marketing Association as a board member and with NorcalBMA as its Product Marketing Roundtable Manager also helped shape this book in different ways. I would like to thank a few key people who took the time to review preview copies of this book. Their thoughts on the book helped in framing my own work from different perspectives that they brought from their own specific sphere of work. They are Devin Redmond, CEO and Co-Founder of SocialiQ Networks, Rajesh Subramaniam, Senior Vice-President of Global Marketing and Customer Experience at FedEx Services, Porter Gale, former VP of Marketing at Virgin America and author of "Your Network is Your Net Worth," and Gordon Wyner, Chief-Editor of Marketing Management Magazine.
I would also like to acknowledge CalmSea Inc. Co-Founder and VP of Products, Vivek Subramamanian, for sharing information of use to me in writing this book.

Special thanks go to my editor Joanne Shwed who made the whole process of editing go very smoothly and to Pinky Mehta for her effort into cover design. Most of all, this work would not have been possible without the sacrifice from my two kids for understanding mom's lack of availability and who lent their enthusiasm for the book project by participating in choosing its cover design and imparting advice on how to make it successful! I would also like to acknowledge my husband for his support throughout the writing of this book in many ways.

Contents

Figures and Tables

Purpose of This Book

Build an Effective Strategy to Transcend Social Media Chaos

Traditional marketers are not sure how to start, where to start, and how much to invest in social media. According to a recent survey[1] of marketers, although 70% are using social technologies, only 3% report deriving substantial benefit from it across all stakeholders. Only eight percent of marketers consider themselves social media leaders. Fifty-six percent consider themselves either a novice or a dabbler. If you are like other marketers, you are drowning in social media noise and chaos. Businesses have simply jumped in without tying social media outcomes to any business objectives.

There are many issues involving social media, such as the proliferation in the number of networks resulting in fragmentation of audiences, the fact that it is new, and the fact that it requires a very different approach than traditional marketing.

Social media was once called "word of mouth." You now have valuable tools to enable word of mouth online. These new tools are changing the world of marketing and are becoming an essential component in an increasingly digital world defined and marked by sharing.

The purpose of this book is to help you:

- See how social media fits into your overall marketing strategy
- Understand how best to develop social media with allocation among different tools
- Figure out the extent to which social media marketing is right for your business or department given an increasingly digital world of sharing and an empowered customer voice

Whether you are a senior manager experienced in social media marketing or a novice, this book will help clarify how social media fits into your overall marketing strategy, how much you should be allocating given the return on investment, and at what timeframe you should be looking, depending on the specific metrics adopted. This book will help you focus more and understand all the different elements to which you need to be paying attention.

If you are a novice, the glossary and additional resources sections at the end of the book should be helpful.

Social Networks and the Empowered Customer

"Any customer can have a car painted any color he wants so long as it is black."
–Henry Ford, 1909
"I just got my Nissan Leaf, what a drive!"
–Customer announcing to friends on Facebook, 2012

History and the Impact of Social Networks

We have come a long way from when Henry Ford offered us only black cars. It is more than a decade since the Internet arrived and changed business models and the ways in which consumers and businesses interact. Customers can now "pull" information instead of the single-minded "push" of traditional marketing. Amazon™ was a pioneer in its use of the Internet for e-commerce, building the art of selling on top of the Internet and becoming the world's largest marketplace. Now, a large percentage of customers start their buying process online, especially at

Amazon. They read reviews written by people whom they do not know to make up their minds. Thus, has started the beginning of the age of customers persuading other customers.

Marketers today are dealing with a social Web in which customers persuade or dissuade other customers, as opposed to a Web of sites..

Looking back historically, the impact of social networks is not new. Five centuries ago, Martin Luther figured out the importance of social networks in spreading his message of religious reformation faster and wider.[1] When the printing press came along, he found that it was easier and less expensive to print pamphlets. Such pamphlets were easier to share and more likely to be printed by a network of printers. The pamphlets had an important message that helped people understand they were not the only ones feeling discontented. These pamphlets helped them find a similar voice about something they felt uncomfortable about voicing individually, giving them the courage to share.

Soon after, Luther started printing more "visual" information that he felt was more effective. The pamphlets then urged those reading them to share and have discussions with others. This led to Luther's opponents printing their own pamphlets to spread their own points of view and counter Luther's growing influence.

Twitter, the Printing Press of 21ˢᵗ Century

Fast forward to 2010, and Twitter has the same impact as the printing press once had. Twitter was not the cause of revolutions; however, it became famous due to its real-time information that catalyzed and supported revolutions. It is a helpful tool because it can easily shorten messages and do so relatively anonymously. It is also a broadcasting tool with minimal cost, except for time involved, which unfortunately is its undoing in its current form since it also results in a lot of noise.

Today's digital tsunami of information is making customers as well as marketers search for ways to be more efficient and effective. As a marketer, you want a way to handle the information overload while keeping in touch with what is happening in the world. Twitter has provided a venue for those short, real-time bites so you know what is happening in the world around you; however, the ease with which you can "tweet" has also led to a tsunami of tweets. In order to be noticeable, you need to tweet more, which adds to the problem of information overload. This is representative of what is happening in other social networks as well.

PARALLELS BETWEEN TELEVISION AND TWITTER

The history of television broadcasting looks similar. The first advertisements were entertaining; soon after, inundated by advertisements, people simply tuned them out to protect their cerebral cortex from crumbling. Twitter and other social networks are reaching that point a little faster. After all, how many people sit in front of the computer, looking at tweets all day?

Television did not make companies successful. Their creative strategies in using it made them successful. Social media is the same way. It is a channel. Success depends on fundamental marketing principles.

The real trend in today's marketing is the multi-tiered model of communication among customers. In this model, you hope that a "like" or a "tweet" for your marketing communication or product will eventually find its way to a larger proportion of your target market.

In that respect, for marketers who can spend on traditional media, the significant cost barriers to entry give an edge to continue using traditional media and leverage Twitter through, for example, promotions that are only going to be tweeted. Social media has low barriers to entry but has a cost associated for success and sustainability. This allows more in the way of small businesses to get a foothold. In that respect, it evens the field for big and small players in the broadcasting world.

The Empowered Customer

Social conversations are becoming a big part of the customer purchase journey. Many customers start the process online. The social Web—as opposed to a Web of sites—has made social conversations a critical influencer of this process. Customers are turning to social networks for serendipitous discovery, supplementing their search for information through search engines.

THE JOURNEY TO SERENDIPITOUS SOCIAL DISCOVERY FROM INTENTIONAL SEARCH

In the last decade, the Internet saw a fast pace of technological changes, leading to changes in how consumers behave. The onslaught of information proliferation in cyberspace brought the search engine as an answer to a problem, especially Google™ with its ability for customers to find what they wanted anywhere in the world. More recently, we are seeing the impact of social networks on the way prospects and customers discover things, which is termed "social discovery"[2] as opposed to "intentional search."

As customers spend more time on social networks, these networks have further proliferated creating greater fragmentation of audiences. This, in turn, is adding more to the noise and making it difficult for both marketers and customers to convey or find useful and relevant information.

Customers can still turn to reviews and recommendations from others like them, which we have always called "word of mouth." Now, there is a new variant that I call "word of mouse." It is a variant because customers are influenced by people close to them that they know well. They are also influenced by those perceived to be "like" them all over the social Web.

Word of mouth has always been very important to companies. What we see today is a multi-tiered form of "word of mouse" in which transparency is important, customer voice is stronger, and marketers need to be subtle while providing something of value to get permission to speak to their prospects and customers.

All of these changes in customer behavior because of social networks are having an impact on marketing. The traditional ways of marketing seem to be a waste of resources when prospects, who are tired of constant bombardment by all types of information, can ignore and choose their focal point of attention. So how has new technology affected marketing?

Transition from Traditional to Digital to Social

Social media networks have added another layer to the ease with which customers can find information: through friends and other consumers, making it easier to find and evaluate information.

This has happened for a couple of reasons. There is a lot more information coming the consumer's way, and even search engines, such as Google, are coming up short in providing the most relevant information.

Google does an excellent job of finding the most relevant sites related to a keyword or a set of keywords; however, how do we know that the customer is typing in the exact keywords that will give them the information they need? This has resulted in people turning to other sources to simplify their own decision-making and as a way to deal with the data and information deluge.

Google's current search algorithm makes it difficult to find many *new* treasures through a search engine simply because they do not appear on the top two pages. *The serendipitous way of finding something valuable* is the gap that social networks are filling in some ways for customers.

Social Technology and Marketing

Today's social Web gives marketers the opportunity to listen in on conversations to which they could never be privy before, but developing a social digital media strategy is not free. It requires consistent sustainable effort, monitoring, tracking, analysis, and responsiveness. This book looks at how to build this process, what it entails, and what the return on investment of implementing such a process will be.

The fundamentals of marketing are the same, but the technological tools that have an impact on these fundamentals have changed, starting with the Internet and email. Bill Gates (Microsoft®) said that if people had once told him that everybody would be advertising their Websites on television, he would have laughed outright.[3] Now, we see Facebook pages and Twitter handles advertised in traditional television advertising.

The keys to building a successful business are still the same: Provide a great product at a great price with other features, such as convenience and self-service, in-person, or online customer service, and customers will beat a path to your door—provided they know about it, of course. All the social media networks are really channels with different demographics, psychographics, and usage patterns. Part of the problem today is that marketers do not have a social media strategy, only tools and tactics. As such, they find themselves at a loss in a new world, transitioning from traditional and digital to one dominated by online social conversations.

We now have an array of tools and channels for those seeking information and those providing information. Many things have changed, such as:

- The tools available to you as a marketer to accomplish your objectives
- The way customers and prospects are going about their decision-making process, which has implications for businesses to change the way they are spending their allocation on different media and the times at which they should be doing it
- The importance of integrating between channels, which are increasingly fragmented and sometimes not entirely within a company's control, such as Facebook pages created by fans, employees, or competitors

For marketers, it is a dilemma to have a fragmentation of channels. Deciding how to use each of these in your strategy and how to allocate resources are critical issues; however, the fundamentals of marketing stay the same. These are to create awareness, interest, and desire to bring them to the Website, make them purchase and repurchase, and have them make recommendations to others. These fundamentals should still be driving your social media strategy.

When developing a digital media strategy, it is important to remember that the latest generation of so-called "social media marketing tools" are, in fact, technological tools to accomplish fundamental marketing tasks. It is clear that social media is here to stay; however, it is simply another tool. It will not replace all marketing media but will significantly affect many other things in marketing.

This book intends to provide guidance and perspective in using these tools judiciously to develop an effective digital media strategy, while keeping these fundamental marketing principles in mind.

What Social Networks and Empowered Customers Mean to Marketers

For many executives who come from a traditional media mindset, these changes can be mind-blowing. This book provides an overview of an all-encompassing, socially digital media strategy that will bring anyone up to speed on the different available options to make decisions on fit, usage, and allocation of resources.

The most important thing you are getting from the social network tools is to build an asset and permission to communicate with your prospects and customers by earning it – referred to today as earned media.

Earned media, is in fact, becoming as —if not more—important than "paid media" in an era of socially digital Web in which most customers start their journey online.

Use of social media as part of your marketing or corporate strategy requires an understanding of creating trust, harnessing the power of collective intelligence while understanding its limits, and understanding the true cost of entry. This book intends to provide a roadmap for developing, monitoring, and maintaining a social media strategy, and the reasons for doing so in a new age of marketing in a world of digital sharing. As said and demonstrated, the tools will continue to change. One or more of these tools could be relevant, depending on your situation.

Chapter 1 Summary and Key Takeaways

■ Today, you as a marketer are dealing with a social Web of sites, with customers persuading and dissuading your prospects.

■ Pay attention to "earned media," which is becoming more important than before, due to its transparency and availability.

■ Develop a social media strategy, not just tools and tactics.

■ The fundamentals of marketing are still important today. Social media just happens to provide you with a new set of channels with its own demographics and psychographics.

Chapter 2

The Dawn of Social Networks

"As of June 2011, Facebook has surpassed Hyves in Holland, Orkut in Brazil, and GREE, Mobage, and mixi in Japan"

"Social Networks—a global phenomenon with local flavors—VKontakte in Russia, Orkut in India, Badoo in France, mixi in Japan, and Wer-kennt-wen in Germany"
—thenextWeb.com

Growth of Social Networking

Social networking has become a fabric of people's online social lives. According to a recent survey by Pew Internet of U.S. adult Internet users, 66% now say that they use social networking sites compared to 34% in 2008.[1] Facebook dominates the social networking space, and 92% who use social networking sites say they use Facebook. Only 18% report using LinkedIn® and 13% use Twitter.[2] Social networking is not just an American trend. It is a global phenomenon with 82% of the world's online population participating in some social network.[3]

Both Facebook and LinkedIn have an international audience; yet, despite Facebook being an eight times larger network, it has only three times the number of members as LinkedIn in the United States.[4]

The top 10 countries are different in each as well. On Facebook, six out of 10 members live in the top 10 countries, and LinkedIn has eight out of 10 living in the top 10 countries. In addition, on both networks, the United States dominates in the size of the audience; however, the United States only represents 20% of the worldwide audience on Facebook and Twitter, whereas it represents 38% of the worldwide audience on LinkedIn.[5] Thus, in some ways, Facebook and Twitter are more of an international phenomenon than LinkedIn, although LinkedIn seems to be catching up.

People are also spending more time today on social networks than on pornographic sites, which was always at the top historically.[6] According to Nielsen data, Facebook is the envy of the industry in terms of the amount of time spent on it, with Americans spending 54 billion minutes on its site in May 2011, compared to less than half that time on Google/YouTube combined, followed by Yahoo!® in third place.[7] The huge difference between the first and second Web properties in terms of the number of minutes spent is remarkable.

Different Users Prefer Different Social Networks

Social networking has become a global phenomenon; however, social networks are not being used the same way or by the same people to the same extent. There are stark demographic and behavioral differences among users of the different social networking sites.[8] Despite the remarkably enviable amount of time spent on Facebook, there are differences in the profiles and behaviors of users of these sites, with direct implications for marketers.

DIFFERENCES IN DEMOGRAPHICS

As Table 2.1 shows, Twitter has the highest proportion of users from 18–22 years old,[9] while LinkedIn has the least, which is understandable given the nature of its value-add which is professional networking. Facebook has a much greater proportion of users 13–17 and 18–24 years old compared to LinkedIn, which has a greater proportion of users 25–54 years old, compared to the U.S. population demographics.[10]

Table 2.1: Differences in Behavior and Usage of Social Networks

Social Network	User Demographics	Usage	Usage Frequency
Facebook	Females: 58% 18-22 year olds: 16% College Graduate: 35%	Sharing thoughts, photos, news, more personal	52% using once a day or more
LinkedIn®	Females: 37% 18-22 year olds: 6% College Graduate: 75%	Sharing professional information	6% using it once a day or more
Twitter	Females: 64% 18-22 year olds: 26% College Graduate: 39%	Sharing personal and professional information	33% using it once a day or more
Google+™[11]	Females: 29% 24 or younger: 50%	Sharing professional information, many are engineers, developers	Used least compared to others here; less than 3 minutes per visit per month on average
Pinterest [12]	Mostly female audience : 82%	Sharing hobbies and photos	As often as Facebook and growing faster

Source: Adapted by Sujata Ramnarayan from PewInternet.org with permission; Note: Pew Internet data is based on survey of U.S. adults only

LinkedIn's user gender makeup is very different from that of Facebook and Twitter. LinkedIn's users are predominantly male, whereas Twitter has a relatively higher female representation. Facebook users, who share personal details and interests such as birthdays and cooking, and whether they are married, tend to be female.

Both LinkedIn and Twitter have a much greater proportion of highly educated users compared to Facebook.

DIFFERENCES IN USAGE

The differences among these sites are not just about greater representation of certain demographic groups. There are also differences in usage frequency. For example, Facebook is used more often daily than Twitter and LinkedIn by a greater percentage of users. As Table 2.1 shows, 52% of Facebook users engage with the platform daily, much more than users of LinkedIn and Twitter.

There are also associations between age/gender and frequency of posts on Facebook. The younger the users, the more they check for updates, post updates, and make comments. Further, women tend to post updates and comments once a day or more, which is much more than men do. Age, as mentioned, seems to be a significant factor as well, with younger age groups posting updates more frequently.[13]

ach social network has different demographics and usage patterns. Choose and focus on a social network where your target market is spending time.

Although the number of social networks has been increasing, each offers something a little bit different. If these differences are not defined sufficiently enough to warrant a differentiated benefit in using it, as seen with Google+, it will not find much success.[14] This is apparent from the amount of time spent on average on each of the social networks as shown in Figure 2.1.

Figure 2.1: Number of Minutes Spent per Month on Each Social Network

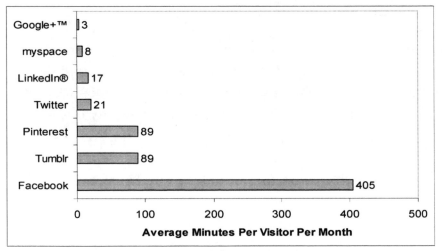

Source: ComScore, The Wall Street Journal

Facebook has the maximum amount of time spent on it and Google+ the least; however, the amount of time spent on a network is not the only criterion for marketing. Various demographic groups for different reasons use different social network sites.

Facebook, for example, is used mainly for connecting with people you know. Twitter, on the other hand, allows for broadcasting to anyone who cares to receive communication from you. Pinterest is visual and nonlinear, and is better aligned for attracting those with similar interests.

LinkedIn has a different demographic group and is better suited to connect with people you have already met professionally, keeping in touch and connecting with people with similar professional interests. LinkedIn differs in its focus on purely professional topics. Pinterest, on the other hand, is aligned with interests such as hobbies. You could call it a "visually appealing combination of Twitter and Facebook."

It is clear that there is room for more than one social network in people's lives. Each of them—or some of them—would be relevant to any company, depending on objectives and the target audience. It is also clear that this fast-changing market has new social networks coming up all the time.

Of all the social networks, in terms of amount of time spent and number of visitors, Facebook and YouTube top the list, followed by Twitter, LinkedIn and fast growing Pinterest.[15] Facebook is different from Pinterest because the audience is sharing things like how they are spending time and what thoughts they are having, as opposed to pinning photos related to interests and hobbies on Pinterest.

Pinterest has positioned itself as a community bulletin board on which your company can "pin" things of interest or allow others to do so. This method has forced companies to think about what they want their brand to stand for in terms of how they fit into their customers' lives and lifestyles. For example, General Electric displays its history through pictures on its Pinterest board.

NOT EVERY CUSTOMER HAS BOUGHT INTO SOCIAL NETWORKS

Contrary to burgeoning evidence of the soaring popularity of social networks and time spent online, data also suggest that there are segments of the population who have not bought into them for various reasons.

A recent article in *The New York Times* by Timothy Egan spoke about the problem of oversharing on social networks.[16] Although Mr. Egan was discussing the problems of saying something you might regret that continues to stay online, or banal remarks about sandwiches people ate, it was interesting to see the number and types of comments his article generated. The comments showed that not everybody likes new social networks, such as Facebook and Twitter. You could segment those who made comments into three segments based on content and sentiment expressed:

■ Those who have positive feelings toward social networks and sharing

■ Those who recognize the positives and negatives and

■ Those who are completely against them because of privacy issues or because they see them as a degeneration of social culture due to loneliness or increased narcissism.

It is clear that people on these networks are different, and not everyone is going to take to social networks or use them in the same way; however, the very fact that so many chose to comment shows our proclivity to sharing our thoughts and opinions with complete strangers when excited about an issue.

This preceding analysis of social conversations about social networks does not necessarily imply that Facebook or Twitter are the preferred networks of choice or that social networks per se are unnecessary. To the contrary, this analysis underlines the need for people to help, comment, and share, which is happening more frequently online, even if it is about the negative aspects of specific social networks.

Social networks are not significant per se, but it is the fact that the Web is becoming a global place for social conversations, whether it is on Facebook or through a simple comment or share feature.

Today, conversations have become a huge part of the Web, hence the term the "social Web." Facebook is indeed a big part of the network, but that is not the only place. In some ways, Yelp® is another social network where people are talking about different companies. Larry Weber, author of *Everywhere—Comprehensive Digital Business Strategy for a Social Media Era,*[17] talks about finding 50,000 general conversations related to shaving, and many of these conversations were in smaller micro-segmented social destinations. As Weber puts it, you cannot slice time, and it is not always clear when one era is ending and another is beginning. The Web has indeed changed.

As the analysis of social comments on *The New York Times* shows, not everyone has bought into social networks, but a good 41% find some benefit in them—as defined and interpreted by them—as Facebook and Twitter.[18] However, just voicing your comments is also about sharing. When seen that way, even those who see Facebook and Twitter as unproductive and degenerate see the value of sharing on the Web.

*T*he Web has indeed transformed itself from a place to find and consume information to a place to create and share information.

This creation of content on the Web could be in the form of thought-provoking and introspective blogs, all the way to the banal, and to other short bites of remarks in the form of opinion, activities, and assistance. These forms all bring value to a social Web.

However, as previous analysis shows, not everyone has bought into specific social networks, such as Facebook or Twitter, although these networks continue to carry a large segment of the sharing. The Web is becoming more social, but not all social networks are relevant to every marketer or to every customer and prospect. This takes you back to the need to identify where your target market is, and that goes back to the fundamentals of marketing.

Social media strategy is not about establishing a Facebook page or a Twitter account. It is about identifying where to find your target customer or prospect and how you can leverage the power of the social Web for your specific business objective. Research shows that even if you find a sizable portion of your target segment on Facebook, not all are using it or using it actively. For example, 58% of a sample of readers of a New York Times article on social sharing is not using it actively. This means that a sizable mass of your potential audience needs a different approach.[19]

Many companies have not had success with social media due to the following reasons:

- Many are at different points in their social media journey.
- Many jumped in without clear objectives.
- It is a new channel, which continues to evolve rapidly.

You can divide companies that are engaged in social media into three segments:

1. Those that have dabbled in it but have done so without a strategy;
2. Those that are still new to it but have instituted a strategy; and
3. A third and smallest segment that considers itself quite experienced –the early adopters

In some ways, the early adopters paved the way by making mistakes and then fine-tuning as they went along, which made it easier for others who followed to plan better.

Part of the challenge of using social media for marketing also lies in the fact that companies are just stepping in to make available the necessary tools to make social communities and conversations an asset to marketers. In some ways, it harkens back to the beginning of the Internet, which allowed for the creation of information. This early system became unmanageable until search engines came along, followed by e-commerce platforms and analytics that offered better marketing advantage.

In some ways, we are at the beginning of the social Web, even though it is still hard to find all the conversations taking place. Tools, such as SocialiQ Networks and Crimson Hexagon, are just beginning to solve the problems that the social Web presents. Despite having a market of 850 million people[20] who readily share personal information, including their profile, likes and dislikes, activities, and location, Facebook still has a hard time monetizing that information. It is similar to how search engines found it difficult to monetize until the idea for "keyword ads" came along. Facebook has similarly started exploring the idea of "personal endorsements" that will be unique to their site.

Despite having all this information, Facebook pages only provide minimal insights to marketers. This information goldmine is only useful to marketers if they use other applications or build Facebook applications.[21] Today, popular Facebook applications are mostly in gaming and other consumer-oriented areas; business-oriented applications are still minimal.

Chapter 2 Summary and Key Takeaways

■ Social networking is here to stay for both marketers and customers, even as it continues to evolve.

■ Different demographic groups use different social networks at different frequencies for different purposes.

■ Companies are at different points in their social media journey.

■ Similar to how search engines came along to solve the problem of information searches on the Web, the tools to monitor and counter the problems for marketers presented by the social Web are just arriving.

Chapter 3

Building a Social Media Strategy

"Successful social engagement is rooted in business objectives—not in a desire to be on Twitter or to build a microsite. Twitter and microsites are tools and tools only with which organizations address business opportunities and challenges."
—*Larry Weber, in book "Everywhere"*

S ocial media is now a critical arsenal in your portfolio of tools to reach your end customer. A recent survey of chief marketing officers shows that most want to increase their share of spending on social media.[1] That is absolutely the right direction, but it is only one direction to reach a fragmented audience overwhelmed by information.

What is a Social Media Strategy?

The term "social media strategy" is one of the most popular searches on Google indicating to the fact that people want to know more about it. The search for this term has doubled to 10 times the average since 2008, when the press first started writing about the concept. It has come to include a broad array of tools such as Facebook, LinkedIn, Twitter, and blogging. Although blogging seems to be more of a communication and conversation tool, users tend to put it in the same bucket as a social media tool.

*T*he reason that blogging is put in the same bucket as a social media tool is that content is a big part of what is curated and shared among social networks. Content - that is timely and timeless - is the currency of social networks.

The definition of "social media" is seemingly hard for most people. In more than 1,000 high-income professionals surveyed by Lon Safko, 66.4% said that they could not define what social media was, but 99.1% said that they knew it would have a significant impact on them and their businesses. Safko simplifies the definition as simply the media we use to be social.[2]

Asking people to define "social" brings different definitions, such as communicating, sharing, community, connecting with people you did not know before, or connecting with people you already know. Many social media tools reflect these differences in its definition, offering features to accomplish the social aspect of the equation in different ways.

This book intends to bring clarity to how these tools address the aspect of social media marketing, so marketers can make better use of them in a way that maps their problems to solutions.

Panelists at a recent panel discussion at SVForum, were asked for a definition of what "social" means. It was interesting how the panelists had no common definition; however, the discussion implied that a social media strategy involves having conversations, monitoring conversations, and building and nurturing a community using the tools built for a social age.

We are now transitioning from a pure Web to a community-based Web. In some ways, we have transitioned from a one-to-many Web communication to one that became pull centric with customers who were looking for information and buying products. We are now moving into another phase of a social Web centered on dialog, sharing, and interactions, of the company and its customers, and customers with other customers (see Figure 3.1). Many tools enable these social interactions.

Figure 3.1: Pure Web to Community-Based Web

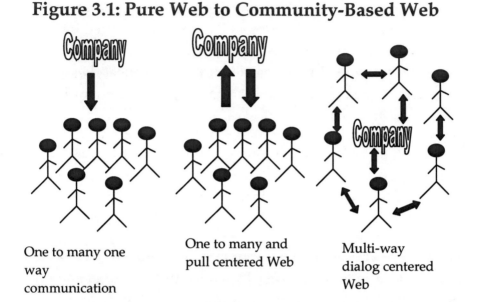

One to many one way communication

One to many and pull centered Web

Multi-way dialog centered Web

Components of a Social Media Strategy

The Website, along with email, were the first technological marketing tools of the most recent times to have a significant impact on communication. They allowed for social interactions faster, quicker, and in a group format much more easily than existing technologies of those times. What has changed recently is the availability of many social tools, such as Facebook, Twitter, and LinkedIn, which make it easier for people to share with many.

Having so many tools from which to choose is a challenge in itself:

■ Do you use tweets as part of your marketing strategy? Who is listening to these?

- Do you maintain and cultivate a Facebook audience? How do you keep them engaged and reading your Facebook updates?
- What about YouTube, podcasts, LinkedIn groups, blogging, SlideShare, whitepapers, and email marketing?
- What about adding Google+ and Pinterest to the list?
- What role does the search engine play in all this?

How does a marketer possibly deal with each of these channels and still be effective and efficient?

Email was the first tool that allowed for faster interactions. As a Senior Analyst at Gartner Group, a global industry research firm, I remember the first few press releases that came through email and how they got my complete attention; however, as many more companies started using that tool, I felt numbed by the amount of information coming my way.

A similar thing is happening today with Facebook. While it might be great to have a friends' circle of 1,000 or more, it is not humanly possible to pay attention to all the information. When consumers adopt different channels, it is an attempt to stay on top of what is happening by depending on others whom they may or may not know to filter the information for them. This is their way of dealing with the information deluge in a time-compressed era.

While fragmentation of channels is a dilemma for marketers, it is also an opportunity to create more awareness in a multi-tiered way through "likes," "tweets," or "shares."

In some ways, this fragmentation is also a result of the way consumers are trying to deal with excess information and to simplify decision making. When customers see a "like" or "tweet," it tells them that they can trust that information and gets them closer to the purchase decision. Using Facebook "likes" or "tweets" through Twitter are tools for companies to increase awareness of their products and services and, at the same time, win a token of trust from prospects.

Twitter is different in the sense that it provides for "real-time" information. While its broadcasting feature has resulted in a lot of noise, it also enables finding real-time information much easier. It is the tool that customers turn to for real-time news, and the tool marketers should use for sales promotion, for example.

YouTube and podcasts point to the way in which customers are dealing with excess information by turning to different media for a break from a barrage of text. In many cases, video is more conducive than text for product demonstrations. This gives companies an opportunity to present information in a different format as a way to reach customers at different times, in different places (e.g., mobile), and in a different mode.

Blogging is another component of the social media strategy toolkit. It is an opportunity for a marketer to build trust and brand personality. It is also more difficult to do than tweeting or entering Facebook updates. Thus, it can give you a competitive advantage with investment of time and effort. It also helps with search engine optimization.

Search engine marketing and search engine optimization are still critical components of your digital media toolkit. Marketing strategy has always had the customer at the center. We are now looking at figuring out what the customer is likely to be *thinking* at the time of the intended purchase.

Central to all of your social media strategy is still your Website. With the use of all of these technological tools, you are trying to solve the fundamental marketing problems of how to get the customer or prospect to:

- Become aware and interested in your product or service
- Get them to purchase and purchase again
- Get them to recommend your product to others.

Social Tools Continue to Change

As evidenced by the disappearance of MySpace, and the recent appearance of Google+ as a formidable competitor to both Twitter and Facebook, these tools will continue to change. Your Website is where you have complete control. Your Website is here to stay for the long term, and it is where customers can get a complete understanding of your products or services. When using these new social media "tools," remember what they really are and that they will continue to change.

Use these tools as technologies to map your fundamental marketing problems to solutions. These tools provide greater context, greater reach, and a way to generate greater trust in your product or service through two-way communication with your audience with permission. In an era in which channels are fragmented and options are many, having an audience with permission to speak to them is a valuable asset bestowed by these social networks.

This trust from two-way communication happens at two levels:

1. When you see a reference or recommendation directly from a friend
2. When you see multiple recommendations from users whom you do not know, such as from customer testimonials

Steps to Developing an Effective Social Media Strategy

An effective social media program means that you start with goals. The steps to building an effective social media strategy, as shown in Figure 3.2, are as follows:

Step 1: Listen

On Twitter, you can do this by using hashtags and search. Hashtags are similar to keywords in a search engine except they require manual insertion. There are other listening tools as well. For example, a search for "Chobani yogurt" on socialmention (a search engine focusing on social conversations) comes up with all mention of the keywords. It also provides other information, such as the keywords used to find the product, the most prominent bloggers and microbloggers, and the frequency of mention.

Figure 3.2: Steps to Building an Effective Social Media Strategy

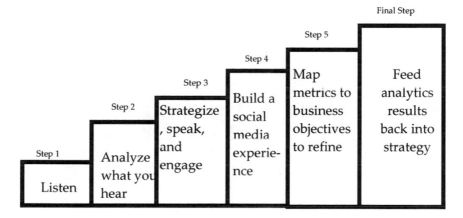

Step 2: Analyze what you hear

This will enable you to make sense of the information. You can extend this listening to competition in order to get a better picture on where you stand. For example, Chobani® yogurt is only a five-year-old company; however, it has spent time perfecting its product to create one so much better than its competition that makes its customers and users its spokespeople. Chobani also has a socially savvy marketing strategy, engaging its community of influencers through blogs and photographs. Extending this listening to its competition reveals that Chobani has the largest share of mind with mention of its brand every six minutes on average compared to less frequent mention of its competition, as shown in Figure 3.3.

Figure 3.3: Frequency of Social Media Mention of Each Brand

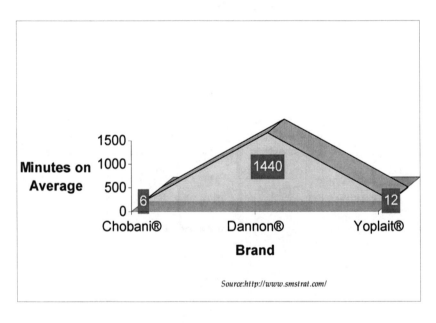

Source:http://www.smstrat.com/

Step 3: Strategize, speak, and engage

Using Chobani as an example again, the company's Website is quite socially savvy. Their social strategy is well integrated with a community-oriented marketing strategy, which involves fitness events sponsorship where they use their product and Chobani-branded t-shirts for additional name recognition. Their Website features a series of "guest bloggers," who write about nutrition and fitness, again using this as a way to engage influencers and their prospects and customers directly.

For its Facebook page, the company uses mostly delectable photographs of Chobani yogurt-infused end-products that are hard not to "like." The sentiment is generally positive, with people from the U.S.'s west coast to Brazil, wondering where or when they can get their product closer to home. Thus, its strategy for engagement is through relevant photographs, a safe and more efficient method than trying to come up with text updates and easier to do for such a consumer product.

Chobani is a small company. For a bigger company, there are other issues when starting the program at the corporate level. Should you have a single corporate voice or multiple employee voices at the departmental level? Do you have only one person speaking or multiple voices? One way to incorporate multiple voices is to have a person responsible for approving those multiple voices while keeping the vibrancy of multiple voices alive.

Developing an effective social media strategy is an iterative and evolutionary process that you should combine with business objectives. Some examples of such business objectives are:

- Increasing awareness for a product (e.g., Chobani has done that quite effectively, whereas Dannon® has failed to do so miserably, despite having a product in the Greek yogurt category)
- Identifying prospects and customers with which to engage
- Getting ideas for innovations
- Improving customer service

■ Launching a new product

Starbucks™ (shown in Figure 3.4) has used crowdsourcing by creating a separate Website with a community that has produced an incredible number of ideas for new products and operational ideas.

Figure 3.4: Starbucks™ Using Online Community for Ideas

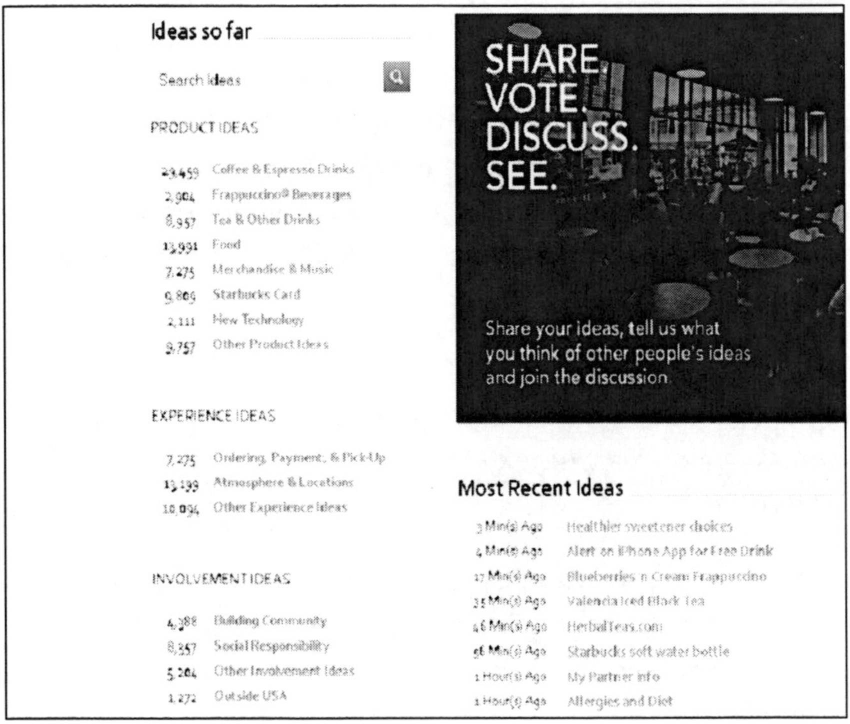

Source: http://mystarbucksidea.force.com/

Pebble smartwatch has used crowdsourcing as a way to launch a new product admirably.[3,4] Having trouble raising enough financing, its founder Eric Migicovsky turned to the crowd-funding Website Kickstarter, offering the $150 watch at a discount for the first 200 who committed to put in $99 each, and thereafter at $115. Within two days, the company had raised $1 million from people pre-ordering the watch. As of mid-May 2012, the company had raised over $10 million from 68,929 people.

This level of engagement pre-production is special because of the comments from individuals who asked about features of the watch, enabling the company to figure out what features to include. For example, they introduced a waterproof watch based on backers' comments. These comments on feature requests continue to pour in, including requests for kinetic motion or solar charging watches, and apps that would make the watch more useful. This is an example of a product that has used crowdsourcing for funding production, idea generation, and, through user involvement, created spokespeople.

Another business objective for using social media could be to *improve partner relations*. SAP, the German company that makes enterprise software has used social media in the form of message boards to create a community of developers who ask and respond to questions. The community has been so successful that it has grown to millions of members from 200 different countries with 30,000 members joining each month. SAP has evolved to include other communities beyond software developers that work with its products. It has also started assigning points to its members based on blogs they maintain, conferences they attend as a way to recognize its members. SAP uses networks such as LinkedIn and Twitter to promote upcoming events, while using Facebook to a much lesser extent.[5]

The value-add provided by any effective social media strategy is content, whether that content is curated or created. The goal for any social media strategy is to create or curate such great content that people will want to share and provide easy ways for them to do so.

However, people want to share something new, hilarious, informative, or touching. The key to content creation is to produce informative, inspiring, or entertaining content. If it is a product, it is also important to get people to review it on third-party sites through encouragement or some kind of reward.

We can draw parallels between traditional media and new social media. Great content has always been important in traditional marketing and for public relations in the form of press releases. Yet many press releases are a yawn, talking about things that do not matter. Great content is now becoming more important and its formats vary, whether it is an effective 140-character line, a two-sentence update, or a full-fledged blog or white paper.

Publicity as earned media has always been coveted by marketers. Earned media has taken on more importance today due to

fragmentation of channels and an empowered customer voice.

Earned media, such as an article by a reporter in a magazine or a newspaper, has always been important in traditional marketing. The same earned media is now taking different forms, such as a "re-tweet," a "share," a "recommend," or a review written directly by customers or prospects.

Step 4: Build a social media experience

This requires thought, depending on the business objective you desire. For example, if you want to build a market for e-readers, create a social media experience in the form of a discussion group on books (e.g., digital books and books with most influence). Make a decision to create a new group or to engage with a group that already exists. For example, a community that already exists for digital books could be the beginning of engagement.

This step also needs a way to get the content started, and there are several ways to do this. Creating content on a regular basis takes time, effort, and creativity. Get many participants involved in content generation. For example, speaking as a board member of a nonprofit organization, each board member needed to come up with five ways that the organization mattered to each member. The board was supposed to select and consolidate five comments for campaigning. Instead, the board members decided to keep all the ones they liked so they could rotate the messages. They further decided that this would also work well for Facebook updates. Whatever the social network, there are ways to generate content, and making it a social effort makes it that much easier.

You can have contests that allow people to engage and create, and get others to create as well. The popularity of games, such as FarmVille™ and Zynga®, points to the benefit of using games to get people to engage more. In both cases, the content generation rests on the users.

Another avenue is to create something that is entertaining, informative and educational, or productive, or provides community support. (Facebook falls into the latter category and is really more of a platform, although a popular platform among some users.) You could do this through content, such as blogs and white papers, or through creation of mobile applications and communities.

One of the reasons for the popularity of the iPhone® is its useful applications, such as for tracking your running, providing tips on favorite hiking trails, or sharing recipes based on ingredients. This requires an understanding of your target market to figure out the best and most useful content and applications.

It has now become customary—especially for those already using these social networks—to find things to share. In addition, when they find something that fits these criteria, they look for a way to express how they feel about it through comments or a way to share through Facebook, LinkedIn, Twitter, or some other network.

Wikipedia® is another example of well-managed, socially created content. Through its collaborative content effort, Wikipedia managed to substitute Encyclopedia Britannica®, which, with its dependency on a select group of experts, could not achieve the same scale and content creation time as Wikipedia.

Initial good content is the spark to lead the way in building an audience; however, after reaching critical mass, it needs sustaining power. Sustaining power comes through social rewards. We are seeing a lot more of these social rewards of recognition to encourage user-generated content and engagement.

Step 5: Map metrics to business objectives to refine

Examine the analytics and refine for an effective social media strategy. Specific measures include looking at the top influencers. Even on Facebook, only 15% of users do regular updates on any average day,[6] yet many log in and spend time perusing, liking, and commenting. Every share gets about 1.1 clicks.[7] Looking at the amount of time spent, likes, shares or whatever the specific measure on that social network would help refine your strategy. To get more data on users, create an app—especially if the community exists on Facebook.

The fundamental shift today is in the way you can measure and track social customer or prospect interactions. Salespeople have always tried to locate the most influential person, who is the center of a hub. Social network analysis now makes it possible to find who is most connected and most influential, to whom they are connected, and how the network changes over time. This is true for product use as well as for expanding product adoption or awareness. Once you have a certain number of users coming to you through a social network, you have the opportunity to trace their individual social networks to move your adoption or awareness level beyond that immediate circle.

The role of "word of mouse" marketing is markedly different today. The availability and use of social tools have made it something to influence, measure, and use in increasing the bottom line directly or indirectly.

Here are several ways in which these social networks may be used:

- For display ads based on more personally revealing information than ever before
- For increasing awareness by having consumers or prospects share your content
- For identifying influencers who can then impact adoption
- For managing overall and disparate social efforts

Traditionally, the roles of marketing, market research, sales, corporate communications, and customer service relations are well defined and demarcated. Different task definitions separate these functions, yet social media affects all. The good, the bad, and the ugly – people share all through different social networks.

As Twitter's power in social revolutions has shown, it is possible to overthrow governments and hurt a company's bottom line when miffed by complaining on Twitter. Although not everyone is on Twitter, it does force transparency on companies just as it forces transparencies on governments. Not everyone is using Facebook regularly, but a significant portion of the population does check in to it quite frequently. This forced transparency also forces customer service to be on its toes.

*S*ocial media intelligence around customer conversations, whether they are your customer or your competitors', can offer a ton of valuable insights to improve your performance.

The general conversations on social networks can yield many thoughts on products and companies, which are valuable as part of market research as well as improving marketing operations. The fact that customers today turn to reviews from known and unknown people makes social media a key for marketing, which has typically focused on paid media. It is possible to extend this to internal social networks as well, so there is more exchange of information among different groups for a quicker flow of information from social networks.

Final step: Feed analytics results back into strategy

For an effective social media strategy, feed the analytics results to improve upon the strategy by looking at how well it is meeting the business objective (in the example used, the objective being to increase the sales of an e-reader).

There are still issues with measurement. For example, if the first connection happens on social media and then the prospect buys on the Web, it is hard to see these connections today. Lack of management and disparate use of social media channels are apparent. You could have one product in your company using Facebook, yet there is no corporate page on Facebook. Human resources could be managing its own social efforts through LinkedIn and /or Facebook. Employees now have the ease and ability to tweet, and there is no control over messaging or positioning. As we reckon with these social media tools as another evolution of the Web, it will become more important to manage social conversations across departments and across products.

There is something to be said about the might of collective effort, collaborative communication, and creation in an age of information deluge. Isn't it time for companies to respond similarly to take advantage of internal (i.e., employee) and external (i.e., customer) collaborative efforts to manage and respond to this information tsunami?

Chapter 3 Summary and Key Takeaways

■ Valuable content, created or curated, is the currency of social media.

■ A successful social media strategy starts with business objectives and listening as opposed to talking.

- Use valuable insights in social media intelligence to improve performance.

Chapter 4

Word of Mouse

A happy customer, on average, will tell three other customers; an unhappy one will tell 11 others.
-Phillip Kotler
Word of mouse multiplies happy and unhappy customer conversations exponentially

Asking Friends and Family—Word of Mouth

What is loosely being grouped as social networks today is an extended and online version of what has always been around: "word of mouth" communication. People used word of mouth communication to find out about reliable products and services and to learn new things. People asked and still ask other people they know about movies, books, and other products and services they liked, and where they bought things. This in turn led to an opinion about their experience, whether they liked it, and whether they would recommend it. This form of communication still happens today despite the availability of social networks.

Anywhere from 40% to 70% of people rely on information from friends, family, and relatives about purchases they make.[1] The greater the uncertainty and risk associated with the purchase, the greater the reliance on people known to them. For example, 53% of moviegoers rely on recommendations from friends; however, 70% of Americans rely on the advice of others when selecting doctors.[2] Given the ease with which we can now find reviews and advice from different networks to which we belong, one could extrapolate this to be 100% in some form or another in today's digitally connected world of sharing.

Since sociologists and marketers recognized word-of-mouth communication as a specific phenomenon, marketers have tried to figure out ways to influence the process; however, it was also recognized as something not easily measurable or in control. It is useful to understand how word of mouth works, how powerful it can be, and how similar or dissimilar it is from "word of mouse," which describes all online interactions between consumers and prospects (interactive comments generated can also be seen as an influential word-of-mouse component) or on specific social networks.

The first thing to recognize is that word-of-mouth or word-of-mouse marketing by itself cannot bring success; however, negative word of mouth does kill a business slowly. Research shows that a satisfied customer will generally talk about a business with three other people, but a dissatisfied one will tell 10 times the number of people.[3] As evident from the opening statement, and the previous one, research shows many different numbers in terms of average number of people told when satisfied versus dissatisfied. However, all research is consistent in terms of how dissatisfied versus satisfied customers behave. This means that it is more important to stop negative word of mouth and address negative word of mouse. Negative word of mouse multiplies tenfold in an online world of sharing that requires microseconds of clicks.

Managing Word of Mouse

If there are people tweeting because of their dissatisfaction with a product or company, it could be exponentially more harmful than ordinary negative word of mouth. On the other hand, if paid attention to, it is possible to harness it in a positive way. As Steve Fuller, V.P. of Marketing at L.L. Bean® admitted to the Wall Street Journal recently," it would have taken months and months before to figure out if there was anything wrong with the product through returns."[4]

Companies today are using these social media conversations as real-time feedback to help suppliers bring product improvements into the market faster. Negative word of mouth typically indicates deeper problems, especially when seen many times. Whereas ordinary negative word of mouth kills a company slowly due to problems that need addressing by management, there is an opportunity to identify such patterns today. However, identifying such patterns is no good unless management recognizes deeper issues of products and processes that could be causing such a negative pattern to appear in the first place.

As my research indicates, not everybody is tweeting, nor has every prospect and customer bought into the idea of expressing every thought on a wall in a social network. It is essential to make sense of the cacophony and weigh each comment properly (i.e., not representative of all your segments, or as something to investigate to see if it carries across all segments and is indicative of a deeper problem).

A number of things make managing word of mouse easier than managing word-of-mouth communication. Typically, your customer base segments itself into prospects, customers, repeat customers, and evangelists or champions. Ideally, and if a company is doing a lot of things right, your segment of champions will drive more positive word of mouth.

Research also shows that your best customers are not always the ones saying positive things. Your low revenue customers may bring you more referrals.[5] Thus cultivating those who say positive things online even if they are not large revenue customers is important. In addition, not every intention to say something positive actually translates into action. In fact, only half of those who say they will make a recommendation will actually do so. Therefore, it is important to provide incentives to increase the rate of conversion from intention to action.

If you have a sizable segment of unhappy customers in an offline environment, it is usually not easy to spot except through declining business; however, if they are complaining on social media, then it should be easy to pick up.

Here are some steps to defuse any negative situation:

- Acknowledge that the customer is unhappy.
- Point out that you are glad they brought it to your attention.
- Explain the steps you are taking to address the issue.[6]

In social networks, how personal you get with the steps depends on the particular situation.

Many businesses fail to make word of mouth work for them because they do not start by providing great customer service or products that exceed customer expectations. Most businesses try to have as many services or products as possible in the "good or adequate segment." Those who experience the negative tend to talk more, those who experience great service tend to talk less, and the majority in the middle says nothing.

Online, this typically translates into more reviews from those who are most disgruntled, and those who are most happy. Numerically, the disgruntled would outnumber the happy for most businesses, which makes it more important to reduce the possibility of negative experiences. As Jerry Wilson[7] points out, this cannot happen unless it is part of the company ethos ingrained as a mission followed by action.

I n a world of digital sharing in which word of mouse can be tracked, generating positive social

conversations should be part of the company mission.

Most companies do not make "generating positive word of mouth" a part of their mission. In a world of marketing where sharing and reviews are the norm, this should be a specific goal.

Generating positive word of mouth or word of mouse requires the same principle of great customer service and a superior product. This has to happen from the ground up through action and words, and not just words.

You can replicate a number of things in the online world from the offline world. First, only four percent of your customers will come to you directly to complain.[8] The rest will simply walk away but will complain to others. Thus, the four percent who come to you to complain are valuable.

The four percent who come to you are also typically loyal customers. Thus, if you can use social media to hear directly from them and address their concerns directly, it gives you an opportunity to save the rest of your customers. Also, given that your champions usually are fewer than others but more important, you could choose to use different strategies to address the complaints or negative talk from different segments differently and generate positive word of mouse, just as you would in an offline world.

In addition, only 10% of consumer-to-consumer communication about brands is happening online; the rest of the 90% still happens offline.[9] Although word of mouse is an important variation of word of mouth, it is not the only component. Word of mouse can be tracked, researched, used as a learning tool, and managed to some extent. The tools we have are just tools. Online tools do not make word of mouth happen; the fundamentals need to be in place.

Most conversations are about three things:

1.   Themselves and others, things they did, things they ate, books they read, movies they watched and so on.

2.   The products they use, intend to purchase, or have heard about

3.   The services they use, intend to purchase, or have heard about

People talk about products and services because that is part of what happens in life; however, rarity largely determines the value of things.[10] People tell each other about what is new, what is great, what is useful, and what the worst is absolutely. At least that is what they value. Lately, Twitter has changed this somewhat with people tweeting constantly. However, as research shows, only 36% of tweets are useful for any particular individual, the rest are either OK or annoying.[11]

People do not care for or to talk about three things:

1.   The boring or annoying
2.   The ordinary and the complaints about personal lives
3.   The common and what they already know

It is clear that, in order for people to talk about you, you have to provide something innovative and interesting, and something that makes people happy. Providing something that makes people unhappy will also get them talking, but that is easier to do. It does not have to be expensive either.

Most customers expect a minimum in customer service, such as the phone answered when called, yet none of us today experiences it among companies in the United States. Most consumers are smart enough to go online today to resolve anything that can be resolved easily, yet companies make it excruciatingly hard to talk to a representative for problems that might not be ordinary.

A couple of examples, which do not cost an arm or leg, depart from this ordinary and poor customer service:

- While you are waiting, the phone message from Geico® clearly says that they understand your time is valuable and, if you do not want to wait, you can get your transaction done on the company's Website. This clear message acknowledges your time as valuable while providing a solution, which makes you feel less impatient. The wait for a customer representative is also never too long.
- Southwest Airlines allows you to leave your number and they actually return your call, which is unusual in the world of customer service.

Using Facebook pages to create a community of "likes" is fine, but research shows that most customers will only follow less than 10 brands, with the majority following one to four.[12]

Presumably, these brands are unique to those who follow them for a reason. Buying Facebook "likes" through discounts might be a good thing to stay in their radar and continue to communicate with them; however, being "liked" does not necessarily convert to positive word of mouse unless there is a strong, positive motivation for the "like."

Some companies promise to get 10,000 fans for a price. This is clearly not a very good strategy for creating positive word of mouth. It may even backfire if the foundation for positive word of mouth is not strong. Others offer discounts and promotions for likes. While this is a viable strategy to get more people to like your Facebook page, it does not help you in the long term *unless* you have something of value to offer in addition to the initial discount. Additionally, 40% of U.S. Internet users stated that their motivation for liking a brand or company was to receive discounts or promotions (See Figure 4.1).

If we look at the statistics in Figure 4.1, you can distinguish between three types of "likes":

1. Those stemming from commitment and strong brand liking ("committed likes")
2. Those "bought" for discounts and giveaways ("discounted likes")
3. Those that clearly mean nothing ("fake likes")

Figure 4.1: Motivations for "Liking" a Brand, Company, or an Association on Facebook

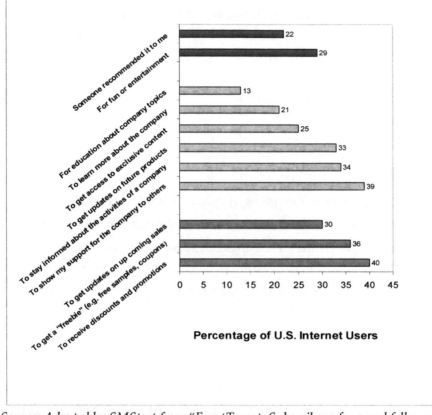

Source: Adapted by SMStrat from "ExactTarget: Subsrcibers, fans, and followers: Facebook X-Factors, August 25, 2010," published by eMarketer.com.

Only the "committed likes" actually count in the long term. While you can get "likes" in return for giveaways, these are not likely to be your core brand/product advocates. About 40% "liked" to show their support, but this could have been for organizations with a cause. Although it counts as a "like" of commitment, it is potentially, overstated in the context of brands and companies. Even if you decide to buy these "likes" in return for either immediate discounts or information about future sales, it is important to distinguish between "likes" that are "bought" for discounts and giveaways and those real "committed likes" that "like" to stay informed.

This latter group is likely to be your core group of advocates for generating positive word of mouse. If you decide to lean toward "discounted likes," make sure you have something of value to offer. "Likes" for discounts and giveaways can be a strategy for increasing awareness and your fan or follower base; however, ultimately without value, most "likes" mean nothing in the longer term. In other words, not all Facebook "likes" are equal.

The other kind of word of mouth, which might be called "amplified word of mouth," is bought by asking customers to "tell a friend" to get a reward. While this might be appealing as a marketing technique, it goes against the norms of social friendships. An alternative might be for both the person and the friend to benefit equally. You may also offer a discount to a friend. Think of word of mouse as "superamplified" word of mouth. Here, we define "superamplified" temporally and exponentially. You can communicate your sharing to many more people much faster than you can offline.

Andy Sernovitz, author of *Word of mouth marketing: How smart companies get people talking,*[13] remarks that word-of-mouth marketing has always been the most important and least expensive source of new customers. It also means that if you are good at keeping your customers and having them come back, they act by default as a source of new customers.

Before you start using social media tools, you should have a solid foundation in products and processes. Otherwise, be prepared to hear what you fear and take the steps to fix it.

Social media marketing can help create greater awareness, but such awareness is of no use if the company has a shaky foundation. This is because some unhappy customers will share. View this as feedback to strengthen the foundation. Alternatively, you could wait and strengthen the foundation before employing these social media tools. At the very least, you should have someone monitoring and listening to the conversations and mentions about your product or service, if any, to respond and use the feedback.

Participation in the online social conversation about you in a way that puts the company in a better light is the minimal level of participation required today.

In a world defined by sharing, consumer reviews, and comments, many opportunities exist for customers to talk about you. These come in the form of blogs, simple product review sites, related communities, and indirect or direct mentions in articles of publications. These various forms need management and enhancement. However, it starts with the basic requirement of customer goodwill.

Any blog or story shared includes an implicit or explicit endorsement or a disagreement, or results in many interactive comments visible to both active and passive participants of the commenting community (i.e., those who are reading and are influenced). Like it or not, the word-of-mouse component of word of mouth is happening online. It used to take place offline and was considered un-manageable; however, we now know that we can get a glimpse of what prospects and customers are saying and take steps proactively rather than reactively.

Proactive steps would be to address word of mouth in general, so your interactions with customers end up in positive endings giving them something to share and talk about—of their own accord. This type of organic word of mouth is stronger, akin to a Facebook "like" that comes from a strong brand evangelist. It happens because that customer is happy to find something exceptionally good about the product and wants to be the one to share it.

Crayola and Revealing Word of Mouse

An example of the impact of word of mouse, and what marketers could learn from it, is how Crayola introduced a new product called "Bubble Launcher." A Google search for this product brings up a result at the top as the product in stock at Amazon with 87 customer reviews and an average rating of one star (see Figure 4.2).

Figure 4.2: Search Results from Google for "Bubble Launcher"

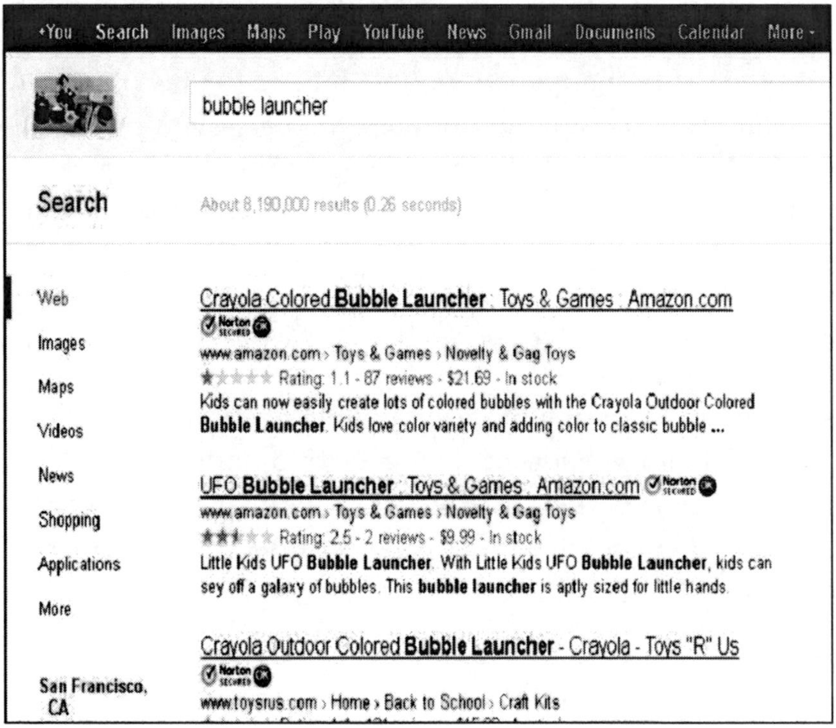

As a parent prospect, if you click on it to read the reviews, this is what you would find:

- Worst product since thalidomide
- Nice idea, terrible execution
- MESSY, will never buy again
- BAD, BAD, BAD
- HORRIBLE
- Do not buy or use this product
- Broke within five minutes
- Do not buy

… And the list of negative comments goes on and on. When reading the comments in detail, it is very easy to see that Crayola has introduced a product that does not work as promised. The bubbles are colorful—a little too colorful—because they splatter and the color is not washable as promised.

The positive aspect of these negative comments is that Crayola has immediate feedback on all the problems with its product. The negative is that no parent reading these reviews will buy this product. In fact, one reviewer goes on to say, "Shame on you, Crayola! I trusted your name. This product is horrible!" Here is an issue of not delivering as expected, which has nipped away slightly at the trust equity that the Crayola brand has built over time.

As this example shows, what customers are saying can reveal a lot about your operations. It seems like common sense that a company should test its product before it launches. They could have done this by asking employees to take the product home for their children. If they had experienced the same thing as real customers, they could have avoided the cost of failure of the product, in addition to erosion of trust and faith in the Crayola brand name.

*W*hat *social media conversations can teach you can be revealing about lack of processes, checks, and priorities in place internally.*

This also explains the fear that many companies feel about employing social media as part of their strategy because they are afraid of what they might hear from their customers and noncustomers, which could potentially reveal internal weaknesses (e.g., shoddy customer service, products not delivering as expected, or irresponsible governance issues).

Today, it is true that customer attention is as fragmented as the number of channels a marketer can pursue. The one thing that is most reliable and getting more important in an age defined by online sharing is word of mouse. Most customers are beginning their journey online and sharing what they like through email, LinkedIn, Twitter, Facebook, and many other online tools.

In many cases, the article that is listed as the most shared article or topic through email will get more clicks, making it even more popular, and somewhat similar to how search engines have become in self-fulfilling a digitally determined order of results. The ones at the top of search results get the most clicks and therefore become more popular. Currently, unlike email, there is no way to see what has been the most "liked" or tweeted, although with the latest announcements from Google, this is beginning to count in the display of results.

If you have a good product and feel strongly about it, encourage your customers to share reviews where they matter. This is true for business-to-business marketers as well and takes the shape of white papers and newsletters. Make yourself known to bloggers who matter to your target audience. At the end of the day, building a strong foundation is necessary to strengthen and make word of mouth possible.

You cannot force customers to say good things about you; however, if they tell you about how happy you have made them, you need to be able to seize that moment. You also need to create the moments to make them happy. This might seem like common sense, yet we do not see every company having great products like Apple® computers, software, or other electronic gadgets that start with a mission of providing benefits instead of features. We do not see a company like Whole Foods Market®, which has a mission to provide healthy, local, and organically produced and unique products, or a retail store like Trader Joe's, about which customers say how they cannot envision life without it—and it is only an "extra" ordinary retail store.

Influencing Word of Mouse

Historically, sociologists recognized the role of word-of-mouth communication in the spread of ideas and products. This was captured by Everett Roger's model of product diffusion[14] to show how early adopters of products tend to be different and lead the way to an early majority of adopters. Marketers used this to identify opinion leaders explicitly, who could then influence their intended target market. In this model of word-of-mouth communication, marketers saw the communication process as influencing an opinion leader, who would then influence other consumers through their expert status. Blogging is the closest tool in social communication that comes close to this model, where the blogger has already established an audience based on some specific interest of mutual liking.

However, not all types of social communication today fit this model of word-of-mouse communication. Social networking sites, such as Facebook, are different because you have one consumer communicating with many, essentially changing it to an online discussion or social conversation about a product based on relationship, however loosely tied. Unlike word of mouth, which could not as easily be influenced or tracked, marketers can now track it over a longer period. Instead of inviting reporters from major newspapers or publications to a news conference, hoping to influence them to write a positive story, marketers now have the option to try to influence bloggers in larger numbers; however, it is not the same as influencing a reporter.

In a study of bloggers,[15] who were approached with the offer of a free MobiTech phone by Buzzablog, the success rate of getting the bloggers to write about the product was as high as 80%; however, there were some differences. Unlike a newspaper that is looking for stories to interest its audience, bloggers wrote implicitly or explicitly about the conflict they experienced in becoming a product reviewer for a company.

They all handled it in a way that would appeal to each of their specific audiences. For example, one of the bloggers made fun of his own product review as though he were selling out, but did end up covering it. Another blogger, typically writing about struggles and victories with Crohn's disease, wrote about receiving a free phone for review as a positive incident in her life.

Although the bloggers wrote in their own narrative style, they all expressed the conflict they felt in writing a product review blog; they felt they had been "bought" to do this type of blog while trying to reconcile the tension between the communal nature of blogging and the commercial nature of a product review.

This shows that bloggers, unlike newspaper reporters, come with a very different mindset. At least at this time, many feel they have a different contributory role to play with trust and relationship between their readers and their blog.

In the example of the MobiTech phone, the marketers approached the bloggers with specific parameters: They did not have to write about it, they could do a positive or a negative write-up, and they could disclose that they were approached to do such a blog. This approach resulted in over 80% success rate. It also underlines the different approaches one would take with reporters versus bloggers.

The bloggers' approach fit into many different segments. It resulted in unique messaging for the product wrapped in the bloggers' own narrative style. Marketers have the option of approaching specific bloggers who fit their target market profile and intended theme of narrative closer.

As the authors of the study using MobiTech put it,[16] we are in a new age of networked co-production of marketing messages and meanings, many of which will not always be only positive. Marketers have to look for engagement, persuasion, and interaction in this networked co-production of marketing messages that not only leave an archive but also can continue as conversations in some format for an extended period.

In case of MobiTech, some of the bloggers talked about it for months in some other context, such as photos taken or in comparison to another product (e.g., an iPhone). This could happen in blogs. In other social networking formats, such as Facebook, the messages do not last as conversations but instead have the potential to spread wider and faster if they catch on. Thus, not all social networking avenues have the same result.

The unexpected makes people excited and gets them to share. Of course, some may perceive social networks, such as Facebook and Twitter, as oversharing and a yawn. That is the messenger and message's fault, not the tool per se. These are tools to use, but the shared message needs to get others excited or to act. Twitter did not cause the revolution in the Middle East. It is the people with a passion and a vision for change. Twitter just provided them with a handy tool to broadcast to the masses worldwide.

To share something in a positive way, it needs to humor, please, or engage through uniqueness or passion. According to Simon Cleft, Global Chief Marketing Officer of Unilever,[17] when TV came along it was much simpler. It was a new medium and you just had to learn to manage it. Fragmentation of media, as with social media, has given consumers a powerful voice, which requires extraordinary imagination and creativity to capture their attention. However, when you do capture their attention, the return on investment is phenomenal. An example is the Dove® ad called "Evolution," which reached 140 million people with an outlay of $100,000.

To achieve word of mouth or word of mouse, social media tools provide a way to implement tactics; however, an innovative and customer-driven strategy still needs to drive it.

The elements necessary for a successful word-of-mouse outcome are similar to those required for a positive word-of-mouth outcome. Some of these elements, whether conducted online or offline, are the following:

- Provide something unique.
- Provide service with a smile.
- Thank customers in a unique way.
- Think out of the box.
- Innovate continuously and incrementally.
- Cultivate those who speak for you.
- Ask your customers what you can do to innovate.

The biggest boon of cultivating a community of evangelists and nurturing them is not just to get more referrals but also to get ideas on ways to innovate. Many new uses for products often come from your customers. A classic example is that of Arm and Hammer®, which started as baking soda and soon found its product used for many different things. Ideas can come from your customers on processes as well, such as customer service.

The problem with creating organic word of mouth is that others will soon follow or imitate, but the simple yet difficult ones are not so easy to emulate. Take the example of Southwest Airlines. They started as a no-frills airline, which, by itself, was unique at that time. They were also unique in having a different way of boarding with specific seat assignments. This was not exactly an asset, but customers did not mind.

The unique aspect of the airline is the flight attendants' humor. No matter how bad the service, their sense of humor stayed intact. Lately, they have a lot more competitors in the no-frills space, so that aspect does not make them unique anymore, but the sense of humor displayed by their flight attendants still does. If you like a joke, you are likely to mention it to someone, and that could lead to mention of the airlines as well. This sense of humor is out-of-the-box innovative thinking that is simple, yet it differentiates them enough to be likely fodder for word of mouth and word of mouse.

Advantages of Word of Mouse

Word of mouse has some significant advantages over its parent word of mouth. This is already apparent with terms currently used to monitor online social conversations. Although it is nothing more than an analog of "search," the term used is "listen." You take the time to "listen" to conversations pertaining to your product and keywords associated with your area of interest to keep a finger on the pulse. This is a significant difference between word of mouth and word of mouse.

Whereas you could not track word of mouth as easily, what is written online stays recorded in cyberspace and can be picked up through a variety of "listening" tools.

Google Alerts™ is a tool that can be set to notify within minutes of something posted online. This gives you the ability to track and respond. Other tools include Radian6™, Lithium, Technorati™, socialmention, Klout, and Raven. There are many more, but these are often mentioned by users (word-of-mouth popularity). (For a list of "listening" tools, please refer to the Glossary and Resources section.)

Word of mouse is also different from word of mouth because marketers can take part directly, initiate, and listen to the conversations. Unlike mass media, where consumers cannot respond, social media or word of mouse allows consumers to react quickly. These reactions may not be what the company expects or hopes to hear.

An example of social media gone wrong is McDonald's™, which created the hashtags #McDStories and #MeetTheFarmers, in order to promote its newly found focus on healthy ingredients. The tweets were followed with tweets from Twitterati, such as:

#Every burger at McD's contains "pink slime," a mix of abhorrent cow part trimmings treated with ammonia. Let's dinner! #McDStories

#creamy chicken McBites ??? Did I hear that commercial right?? YUCK!!! #McDStories

#The moral of #McDStories: people don't start liking you just because you suggest a way to express their admiration.

The last tweet expresses the sentiment and misunderstood use of social media. Multinational corporations, used to creating multimillion-dollar campaigns, can make mistakes when using social media the same way as traditional media. Expect a response. Your audience on Twitter consists of all types of people. You are broadcasting to all of them with a difference: They can react and respond.

There were other tweets about McDonald's social media campaign gone wrong and lessons learned—hardly the position in which a company wants to be. Overall, there was double the number of negative mentions as that of positive for McDonald's, underlying the need to get customers to believe its message. As a Times article reported[18]

McDonald's social media campaign gone awry is a lesson to all marketers as summed up by a tweet: "Note to self: If evil, don't do social media."

Use social media to fix problems before you expect a spread of goodwill sharing among your potential and current followers. To rectify its blunder, McDonald's followed up with another campaign called #LittleThings, talking about everyday tasks that make your day better, such as that cup of coffee.[19, 20] Safer and more in tune with its brand image today.

Chapter 4 Summary and Key Takeaways

■ Today's Web of social networks, built upon social conversations, has always existed as invisible word-of-mouth communication.

■ Satisfied and dissatisfied customers talk, but dissatisfied customers talk more, and this can multiply much more online. However, remember that the vast majority are silent but lurking and influenced despite their silence.

■ Make generating positive word of mouse part of your mission to succeed in a world of digital sharing.

■ Use social media conversations to fix your processes, lack of checks, and internal priorities.

Role of Community in Social Networks

Facebook has provided a platform on which it has built the world's largest community.

Companies need to use such platforms to build a social media asset — a community of their customers.

Building a Community

One of the reasons people turn to the Internet is to associate with people who have similar problems and interests. This could be as simple as sharing feelings and trying to find empathy or create something that is of some significance. It could also be deleterious because some cults can be defined as "communities with a purpose."

Social networks, such as Facebook and Twitter, provide the platforms for such communities to develop. Facebook started with the purpose, "What's on your mind today?" Since then, it has enabled formation of its Groups feature, but this is not new. Email technology had already allowed the formation of groups such as Yahoo! Groups. Therefore, technology-enabled social networking is not a new phenomenon that started with Facebook.

However, Facebook and Twitter have scaled it to a level never before seen. In some ways, they are still platforms waiting for users to find a purpose. These platforms enable the promise of communities. Facebook as a community serves the purpose of keeping in touch. Twitter serves the purpose of connecting with others with a similar interest. It has also evolved into a content distribution platform, yet they are not communities until the platforms, led by a leader of vision, are used.

Wikipedia: A Community with a Difference

Wikipedia is an example of a community with a difference. Built on the Internet, it serves as a social network platform. This distinct community, which has a purpose and clear guidelines, has done a phenomenal job of creating something that, from the perspective of return on investment, is extraordinary. As reported in the *Guardian* in 2004, "The current Encyclopedia Britannica has 44m words of text. Wikipedia already has more than 250m words in it. Britannica's most recent edition has 65,000 entries in print and 75,000 entries online. Wikipedia's English site has some 360,000 entries and is growing every day."[1]

Wikipedia is a nonprofit foundation and according to its founder James Wales, has approximately 200 regular contributors.[2] Every now and then, some errors creep into its content, and one of its regular volunteers notices them right away. The negative aspect of Wikipedia's community-oriented content development is that it is a constant work in progress. Wales, by his own admission, says that they are looking for ways to improve its quality.[3] However, for an international collaborative venture on a shoestring budget, by any stretch of the imagination, it is a phenomenal success.

Wikipedia does have a leader with a vision, but this leader nevertheless realizes that he needs to be more hands off than hands on for the venture's success. Contributors settle conflict resolution issues or they are elevated to a committee, with Wales stepping in as a last resort.

To build a community, there needs to be a leader with a vision. The vision ends up attracting people of like minds, who then are willing to do what it takes to realize that vision. Conflicts are part of the process, and procedures are required for resolution of such conflicts.

Open Source Software Movement

Wikipedia is the second of two major examples of a successful collaborative creation. James Wales actually had the idea for Wikipedia while looking at the work of Linus Torvalds. Torvalds introduced the concept of building an operating system (Linux®) through the free voluntary work of many software developers. As Eric Steven Raymond puts it in his upcoming book, the software community always regarded the development of major software, such as an operating system, as sacrosanct, like a cathedral. It considered it as something that needed building by master craftspeople in secrecy.[4] The concept of software development that Torvalds was introducing seemed more like a bazaar in which there were many voices and completely open.

Yet, there was a method to this seeming disorderly process. Torvalds had a vision that motivated its developers: to provide an operating system that was free and better than one from dominant Microsoft. The open community had both developers, who were coders, and then many beta testers, who tested and reported bugs. Another Torvalds policy was the concept of many and frequent releases. This made it difficult for commercial users of the product to keep track of the versions, but it also ensured early and easier detection of bug fixes.

Eric Raymond tried to emulate Torvalds's success with Linux with his own "Fetchmail" project. He suggests a number of reasons for the success of his efforts in employing a community of users to make a better product, one of which is that he started with a basic concept. In his own words, "When you start community-building, what you need to be able to present is a *plausible promise*[5]." Linus Torvalds took Unix® and presented it to the community; Eric Raymond started with another open-source utility software. He attributes some of his and Torvalds's success to the fact that people looked up to and liked each.

People perceived Torvalds as a nice person that they wanted to help. By self-admission, Eric Raymond is "an energetic extrovert who enjoys working the crowds." As he puts it, "In order to build a community, you need to attract people, interest them in what you are doing, and keep them happy about the amount of work they are doing."

Appreciation goes a long way, as Raymond asserts, "If you treat your beta testers as your most valuable resource, they will respond by becoming your most valuable resource." Another key ingredient, he affirms, is having a leader who has the ability to recognize good ideas from others.[6] In both cases, the resulting product was much more stable, albeit not necessarily innovative.

This is also true of Wikipedia. It is not necessarily innovative since it emulated Encyclopedia Britannica. Linux was intended as a replacement for Unix and later morphed as a replacement for the Windows[7] operating system. In other words, both did something that could not be achieved outside of a community: scale in development and betterment of an existing idea.

Yelp and Angie's List: For-Profit Communities

Another example of a successful community effort is Yelp. Of course, it is different from Wikipedia and Linux because of its for-profit focus. In addition, its contributing community members are more "area" enthusiasts rather than driven by a bigger vision, as in the case of Wikipedia and Linux. As such, Yelp has had to do things a little differently. Similar community-oriented sites, such as Insider Pages™ and CitySearch®, have failed, yet Yelp has continued to grow, thrive, and become well known —even in the face of competition from big giants such as Google and Yahoo![8]

In an interview, Yelp's chief executive officer (CEO) talks about how they now have community managers to grow and encourage reviews by its most prolific contributors.[9] Its "elite" cadre of reviewers comes from all walks of life, such as lawyers, engineers, moms, and even an 89-year-old grandmother with a simple interest in food. Unlike Insider Pages and CitySearch, Yelp stayed narrow, building from the ground in San Francisco and starting with local restaurant reviews; now, it has expanded into many categories.

In order to succeed, Yelp targets people who have an interest in contributing such reviews, recognizing their contributions by honoring them with a special elite badge to identify their status. In addition, Yelp brings such groups together offline through parties sponsored by local restaurants, which are happy to do so for marketing reasons. Similar to how Wikipedia found success through contributions from a handful of 200, Yelp's strongest contributors are in the thousands.[10]

There have been some allegations that Yelp has paid its reviewers, at least to get the initial start, although its CEO Jeremy Stoppelson has denied it, stating that they "tried but gave up due to lack of quality."[11] Those in Yelp's elite squad are required to submit at least one review a day to maintain their status. It is clear that a handful of enthusiasts drive the success of communities. These enthusiasts need recognition through non-monetary means and social engagement. Yelp has added a rating system for reviews to increase their quality.

Angie's List™ is a key competitor to Yelp but with a different model. Started by an Indiana woman in 1996,[12, 13] Angie Hicks felt that people would pay for information on trusted electricians and plumbers. She went from door to door, asking people to write reviews in a subscription magazine and call-in service. In return for the integrity of reviews, people were willing to pay $60 a year.

The method in which Hicks built Angie's List carries some commonalities and differences to Wikipedia more than Yelp. Angie's List is also for-profit but not free unlike Yelp. Angie's List has processes in place to prevent review tampering. This takes place by having employees read each review. In addition, members submit the reviews and sign off that they are not working for the company or a competitor. The company also does not allow reviews by any contractor or company nor do they allow any contractor or company to add themselves to the list.

In this case, Angie's List tries to maintain the success of the community by ensuring that they get something in return for their reviews. What they get in return for their reviews is the integrity of the reviews they will use. Angie's List started by focusing on home and lawn-care services, and then expanded to healthcare. Whereas Yelp has focused on mostly eateries, Angie's List has focused on areas with a higher cost of failure, which in turn requires more faith in the reviews and increases the willingness to pay. In this case, the only factor motivating reviewers is that they all benefit from the quantity and quality of the reviews.

Angie's List also provides evaluation criteria for the companies, making sure that reviewers stay within some specified guidelines. The characteristics used to evaluate all service providers include price, quality, responsiveness, punctuality, and professionalism.[14] Most of the users' feedback for Angie's List is positive with a willingness to pay for the information—thus, a loyal following.

Building a Brand Community

While Wikipedia and Linux were examples of successful nonprofit communities, Yelp and Angie's List were for-profit communities. A hybrid of the two is a "brand community," defined as "a community that builds around a brand." This could occur offline, such as at Starbucks or a Barnes & Nobles store. Successful brand communities are not built around a brand; rather, successful community building strengthens the brand. People go to Starbucks for the coffee as well as the experience. Although it is a loosely knit community because Starbucks does not try very hard, it nevertheless creates a feeling of community by giving people a place to work and hang out.

Similar values and interests—or interests in specific skills— bring stronger brand communities together. These community members are more interested in the value-add they get from the community, which leads to greater loyalty to the brand.[15]

People participate in communities for a variety of reasons, such as finding emotional support and encouragement, developing their skills (e.g., Linux), or doing something for the greater good (e.g., Wikipedia); however, the community leads to a strengthened feeling, coalescing around a brand.

A brand does not make a community, but a community makes a brand.

An example of bad execution to create a community around a brand is that of Pepperidge Farm®. They designed Goldfish® branded games for kids, which turned out to be unsuccessful. It then redesigned and built a community to help build resilient kids.

Putting the brand second is an important element of successful brand communities. The most successful brands, such as Harley-Davidson and Apple products, had a successful following because of the many other things they did to bring a group of people together around a single passion. The brand halo "happened" because of the community.

To some extent, some of the characteristics that Susan Fournier and Lara Lee identify in their *Harvard Business Review* article are consistent with the successes of the nonprofit and for-profit communities identified here. Communities need to serve the communities, not the brand. That is a critical element of brand communities as well.

Fournier and Lee affirmed that it is acceptable to have rivalries that ultimately bring the community closer. Although this premise may not apply in case of Yelp or Angie's List, it is definitely the case for Wikipedia and Linux. Wikipedia stood up to its pricey alternative, Encyclopedia Britannica, and the Linux community went up against what it saw as poorly designed, and pricey Microsoft product, although Linus Torvald, the creator had initially started to find a free alternative to Unix.[16] Having something to work against or to work towards in terms of a greater good definitely seems to be an effective ingredient in strengthening a community.

Fournier and Lee[17] also identified the importance of having many different roles rather than "an opinion leader" for building a successful community. Although an opinion leader definitely helps, it is by itself not enough. The authors identify a number of different roles for the same or different people in the community to play for sustaining and strengthening a community as follows:

- Participating to teach others
- Participating for self-improvement
- Providing a safety net to community members for trying new things
- Being a storyteller
- Greeter to welcome new members
- Role model to look up to
- Someone to act as an ambassador to promote and recruit new members

Although different individuals do not need to play these different rules, it is important to have these characteristics embodied and to provide the value-add from such roles. We now have the official position of engagement or community managers as a role in building communities for companies.

Yelp, for example, looks for community managers who are employees of the company to be in charge of parties. These parties recruit new members and bring a sense of community by hosting and taking care of current members. Facebook, albeit being called a "social network," is not a community unless one chooses to provide the elements described earlier that makes for a stronger community. With its loosely defined purpose of "What's on your mind today," it lacks in the creation of a stronger community unless companies make an effort to do so. As such, it is only a platform.

Another factor for success is relinquishing control without abdicating responsibilities. A brand community manager has to participate as a co-creator, providing the right environment and encouragement to nurture and strengthen while ceding control.

This is also true for nonprofit communities, such as Wikipedia and Linux. Wikipedia has a council for mediation when the community cannot settle an issue through proper debate. On rare occasions, James Wells, the founder of Wikipedia, has the last word (a role he plays as someone to look up to, who does not control but exercises his authority in some cases). Angie's List has its own conflict resolution process when members have a problem with one of the contractors found through its community.

As seen throughout this chapter, building a social media asset in the form of a community takes time, effort, purpose, and certain desirable characteristics fulfilled by the same or different individuals. We are beginning to see companies looking to fill the role of a community manager, but the role is still evolving.

Another concept that is emerging as a way to strengthen communities is that of gamification.[18] Gamification refers to a set of specific feedback based processes designed to encourage specific behaviors. Humans respond well to goals and progress measures and rewards tied to those goals. Gamification is about using these processes to bring about desired behaviors. The one example that exemplifies the process of gamification is LinkedIn. LinkedIn has used gamification implicitly to encourage certain behaviors, such as showing the number of connections you have. It makes people want to increase the number of connections. It got so competitive that LinkedIn capped it at 500+. However, it has continued to introduce other rules for desired behavior, such as the bar that shows what percentage of your profile is complete. It continues to add other features to encourage and increase engagement to keep up with the level of engagement seen on Facebook. Any implementation of gamification to strengthen and build a community has to be done keeping desirable outcomes for individuals and the community as a whole.

Chapter 5 Summary and Key Takeaways

■ Digital sharing happens on major social networks defined as Facebook and Twitter, and on specific communities defined by a purpose. To some extent, Facebook and Twitter are really platforms, enabling the formation of communities on a scale never before seen.

■ Successful communities that enable sharing require a leader and a purpose.

■ Companies can build a community, using successful models described in this chapter, or use communities already developed to encourage positive social conversations around their brand.

Chapter 6

Trust and Taste

"Likes' and "follows" are coveted because of the implied token of trust through customer endorsement.

Building Trust through Social Networks

It is not surprising that the concept of "trust" is relevant to three different and related fields of psychology, sociology, and economics—and, by its derivative, —business in general. In all three domains, we define trust by several other concepts,[1] such as:

- Predictability
- Reliability
- Integrity
- Benevolence
- Competence

- A given set of standards
- Honesty
- Confidence
- Reputation
- Strength

Clearly, trust is a complex concept driven by many different factors.

In the digital world, trust takes the form of reputation, as evident from composite ratings by other customers who appear on many Websites. We also measure reputation through Klout Scores, described as a function of the number of people you influence in your network, how often they act upon something you post, and the degree of influence of your influencers.[2] In order to compose such a score, ©Klout Inc. takes into account factors such as the number of tweets, mentions, likes, and shares. However, the problem with this approach is that it does not take into account the quality of what is shared—similar to Google and its popularity ranking. Regardless, the number of current followers for an individual or a company is a representation of trust.

For companies that already have an established brand name, it means that they need to be on social networks, building their social media assets and trust as a result. Even though this approach is harder for new entrants, they should use this channel to build social media assets for the longer term. Studies show that familiarity is the foundation and first step toward the process of building trust.[3] To that end engaging an audience through regular posts—through Facebook, Twitter, or some other social network—goes a long way toward building familiarity and, therefore, trust.

Another aspect of digital trust is the reputation of the person making the recommendation. To manage this aspect, many companies have started a rating system of the reviewers or reviews by others who are using it to manage the risk of decision-making. We have always used customer testimonials as a representation of trust. Hearing directly from people known and unknown to you is an even stronger representation of trust, and something that social media networks and communities provide.

Thus, social media reputation management has become a component of trust management for companies. The Website goodreads.com has seen the number of subscribers skyrocket through Facebook because of greater exposure. In some ways, you can think of social conversations, especially positive ones, adding to the trust. The negative conversations provide a way to keep a finger on your customer's pulse to manage trust. Trust is a multidimensional and dynamic concept. The more you have through the transparent social conversations happening today, the better you can respond and manage it in a positive way.

The Fall of Trust and the Rise of Social Networks

One of the reasons that social networks have become popular as a source is the information deluge; the second reason is trust. You trust that, if many people like something, then it must be good—especially because you believe that they are not representing any commercial interest, which may not be entirely true.[4] The more you know that person, the greater the level of trust in the recommendation provided. Also, if you do not know them, just connecting with a human being instead of a generic corporate email or Website contact form makes it that much more human, which comes with a higher level of trust.

When we say we "trust something or someone," we are saying that this person will not knowingly sell something to us that is harmful or unrepresentative of what is being promised. When we see many people who do not know each other but who meet and interact online from a worldwide platform and endorse something, we feel that it shows validation. Statistically, in many cases it does, although it could have a negative impact due to the concept of thinking like everyone else (called "herd mentality").

Why is there a low level of trust in "commercial interests"? After all, isn't commerce interested in getting a higher level of profit by selling something to make their customers happy? Studies show that "trust" in governments, institutions, and companies has declined in many societies. This is due to many reasons, one of which is a more aggressive commercial ethic.[5]

As marketing has become more sophisticated, consumers and

customers who have been bitten by products and advertisements not delivering on promises have also become more discerning.

Some companies are using this lack of ready belief in advertising to their advantage by focusing on "truth-based marketing;" Other companies are trying to get higher scores on corporate social responsibility.

I often use advertisements that my kids like as an opportunity to teach them about becoming more discerning and not believing everything you hear in the ads. In fact, some corporate executives, such as Simon Cleft, former chief marketing officer of Unilever, have discussed problems when trying to do the right thing for society and the conflict they experience with investors who would like to see a higher rate of return in a much shorter time.[6] This situation has led some states to introduce laws allowing the creation of special types of "benefit" corporations that investors cannot sue, so they can better focus on corporate social responsibility.[7]

Do Social Networks Build Trust?

While print, radio, and television allowed companies to reach more people quickly, it also led to the creation of more impersonal communication between the company and its customers. The Internet allowed companies to reach many more people worldwide while adding a certain level of risk for customers because they do not know the company.

Social networks are the tool that customers are using to reduce the risk of loss they face. An individual's endorsement carries a level of trust, just as the endorsement carries a risk to the endorser of losing the value of their opinion due to a wrong or misplaced endorsement.

Using the hashtag #McDStories to focus on its healthy ingredients, the example of McDonald's Twitter campaign gone awry illustrates the lack of trust in McDonald's in its perceived credibility on the aspect of health.[8] It illustrates how trust is a multidimensional and complex concept and how its lack can backfire in a social media environment. It also illustrates how "truthfulness" and "believability" become very important in social media. McDonald's could continue its campaign the next day, using concepts more related to its brand and therefore credible ("feel good").

In learning about the role "trust" plays in social networks, it is useful to look at the rise of skepticism toward anything company related. Public relations did not become a full-fledged field until the 1940s. After World War I, companies hired Edward Bernays, the original orchestrator of prowar propaganda.[9] He successfully used his understanding of psychology to convince the U.S. public to support the war. Later, he convinced American women to take up smoking as a symbol of emancipation.

Today's consumers, subjected to a great amount of spin over the years, have become more skeptical and suspicious of all marketing messages. Marketers, in turn, have had to be ever more creative to beat consumers' skeptical antennae. We can see examples of this marketing creativity in endorsements that resemble word-of-mouth recommendations—even to the extent of hiring people who pose as ordinary consumers. This is one of the reasons that social networks have become so popular; however, they are somewhat new. Overthrown governments, or those in danger of defeat, have also started using social networks to negate the "truth." Since the network is open to anyone, it makes it harder for any institution to block out the "truth." This openness also makes recommendations from your immediate network more powerful.

As marketing propaganda bites consumers, they have become smarter about evaluating messages; however, these tactics have also eroded trust. This makes the messages from ordinary people as evaluators, who do not have a vested interest that is of a commercial nature, valuable to other customers and to companies.

However, vested interests are playing a role in this as well (e.g., false book recommendations on Amazon). As consumers have turned more and more to others like themselves as a way to validate what companies tell them, companies and competitors too are manipulating reviews.[10] Although this type of treatment has so far been limited, it is still rather early in the days of social media. Some companies are placing protective filters, such as rating the rater or the recommender to add to the level of trust.

In their book, *A Question of Trust,* [11] Bibb and Kourdy mention that nearly every business leader to whom they spoke mentioned that trust is important for profitability. They said they knew it, although they could not prove it. The lack of inability to measure the relationship between trust and profitability shows how simple the word sounds but how complex and difficult the concept is in practice.

Consumers say they "trust" an organization or a company, which usually means that they know that the company will deliver what it promises. Consumers trust that Apple products will look good and work seamlessly; however, the latest Twitter campaign gone wrong—when McDonald's started its tweet by associating itself with healthy ingredients and was out-tweeted in turn by disbelievers with jokes— reflects a lack of trust. This lack of trust is about what McDonald's says it is delivering (healthy food) compared to what the company actually serves. Here, there is a clear disjoint between what they say and what they do.

One of the key components of trust is doing what you say, expressing your values, and delivering on it. If "health" is a value you want to promote, then you have to deliver on that value if you want your prospects and customers to believe it. In social media, the feedback is very quick when the conduct and communication are not in sync.

Trust is built—and lost—one customer at a time. It can grow and it can wane. Every good interaction that a customer has with the company builds on it, and every bad experience erodes it. Social networks cannot build trust immediately nor is tweeting going to build it without a customer experience that builds on this trust. However, it gives an open channel for any company to start promoting itself and building on first awareness, which is usually followed by trial. If it is a good experience, customer goodwill and endorsement through social channels will occur.

Traditional companies find social networks discomfiting because it gives anyone—employees, customers, or competitors—the ability to say anything. It is truly not a medium for the old command and control model of management; however, there are positives.

In looking at innovation and company performance, the authors of Question of Trust[12] attribute the Talent Foundation as having identified several key factors important to innovation, which are no different from those required to build trust within an organization. These are the ability for employees to step out of their comfort zone, take risks, and share information through open debate.[13] This is consistent with findings from another recent study by the Human Capital Institute that found a strong connection between companies that achieve strong business results and high ratings in trust, leadership, and collaboration.[14]

Not all organizations have this in-built culture, which is also a part of the culture of social conversations. Not every customer is going to be full of praise and not every campaign is going to go right. It requires a willingness to experiment, learn, and fine-tune on the go.

As the McDonald's "Tweeting Gone Wrong" incident shows, social media is forgiving and has a short memory. According to the chief executive officer (CEO) of Technorati, Ms. Higgins, the half-life of any tweet is four to eight minutes, and the half-life of a Facebook update is one hour and 20 minutes.[15] The conversations can be changed or even acknowledged with humor while changing it.

Trust is built through open communication; however, this open communication can take different formats. Ricardo Semler, CEO of SEMCO, says that, in his company, salaries are public information. He lets his employees set the salary themselves and is surprised at how often they value themselves less.[16] On the other hand, Apple CEO Steve Jobs had a completely different style of keeping secrets in the company; however, there was open communication within this lack of complete flow of information. Employees "trusted" him to treat everybody equally. Employees trusted him to work for a better world. The day they joined the firm, they were told of the dire consequences that would meet them if they spoke to anyone about any Apple products in the works.[17] Thus, Apple Inc. provides a different example of trust building within a context of no flow of information but with very clear expectations and open communication about those expectations.

Despite the lack of open flow of information, Steve Jobs fits the description of Level five leaders, described by Jim Collins in his book, *Good to Great*, as doing the right thing for the company, not for themselves.[18] Although Apple Inc. veers away from the typical model you would expect of building trust, it did carry all the components in a slightly different context. Thus, as long as your communication is consistent and open, and fits expectations created, social networks are useful in building trust.

Why Use Social Networks to Build Trust?

Social networks today give you an opportunity to interact with customers firsthand. Many customers tweet about where they are going or what they just ate. As a company listens to this chatter, you could potentially use it to find out what their experience was like. This of course requires investment in time, effort, and personnel. As *A Question of Trust* states, when kept informed, customer trust increases[19] and this is especially true at difficult times. To that end, social media channels give you a more intimate way to communicate, interact, and respond to your customers as never seen before.

Trust Does Not Equal Taste

Social networks have turned into a way to discover new things and new information. When we see information from a person whom we know and trust, we tend to pay more attention; however, trusting or knowing someone does not mean that we necessarily share the same taste.

This explains the popularity of tools such as Twitter and Pinterest, which enable users to connect or follow them based on shared interests. For a long time, Yahoo Groups has allowed people to connect based on interests. The new social network tools make it a lot easier in the way they help you discover, organize, and create unlike the old-fashioned email-based groups.

Thus, although "trust" is a big component of the value-add a company can build by building a community, taste is equally important. You can incorporate taste in different ways (e.g., by allowing organization around interests, or through a rating and recommendation system as communities such as Yelp and Amazon have done).

Implied Trust Requires Quality Checks

As customers turn to other customers—known and unknown—to help with their decision-making, and as this trust-building takes on greater importance to marketers and customers, the need to evaluate the quality of these reviews becomes more important. For example, some small business owners have accused Yelp of trying to blackmail them into paying to have negative reviews not shown at the top of the list. As marketers and consumers embrace digital and social media, measuring the quality of social media content becomes all the more critical.

Several things happened in March 2012 to illustrate the official turning point, affirming the supremacy of digital media in the future. Proctor & Gamble, the largest consumer products advertiser, said that the focus of its marketing team is going to be on digital media to reduce costs and increase efficiency. Since Marc Pritchard, Chief of Global Marketing for Proctor & Gamble Co. came on board in 2008, several of its products used only digital media to reach its consumers without a budget and did remarkably well.[20] In tandem, the same week, Encyclopedia Britannica took the axe to its historical and monumental print form, officially pulling the curtain on a dying product on which it has been relying less and less for its revenues.[21] In a third incident, Glenn Beck announced that he is starting his own online television network called GBTV. In 2012, he expects to garner $40 million from his Internet channel compared to his $2.5 million salary from Fox News.[22]

Digital and social media are having a huge impact on new ways to reach your audience without intermediaries and at a much lower cost.

This proliferation in social media content has resulted in a proliferation of quantity over quality, or rather the inability to separate quality from quantity among the noise in spite of all the available search tools.

Current Metrics to Measure Quality of Social Media Content

One metric that is used to judge popularity or quality of a source is the number of likes, tweets, or shares; however, we all know that, similar to search engines, it is possible to manipulate these metrics as well. In fact, there are already companies that will buy you tweets or followers.

To overcome this flaw, marketers could measure engagement by the number of clicks to open or continued responses to updates. This method also has a flaw. In the open world of social media, anyone can follow— those who like you and those who hate you. One only needs to look at the Facebook page for McDonald's as evidence. It has a highly engaged and an equally highly enraged social media audience.

You could overcome this bias in measuring quality by conducting sentiment analysis to see what percentage of the comments you receive are positive versus negative. While this would eliminate the quality issue somewhat, the openness of social media is also its Achilles' heel. Most vocal consumers are there because they feel strongly—positively or negatively—about a product or an issue. Thus, while social media may capture the feelings of those most passionate, it fails to capture the feelings of those who may even buy your product or service again, or those who may not be particularly enthusiastic or disappointed with it.

 *entiment analysis in social media only captures the feelings of the most passionate. To make better*

sense of it, you need benchmarking to gauge the volume and trends in volume of positive and negative sentiments.

More Needed to Measure Social Media Content Quality

How trustworthy are the remarks in an open world of digital media, especially as social comments are beginning to have an impact on the rise and death of a product? This is similar to the way that search engines, such as Google, depended on the popularity of a site and page rank to determine the position of a page, which made it valuable in the beginning; however, the Internet audience figured out how to increase links through link farming to affect simulated popularity. One can easily see social media also going in this direction.

According to a study by Michael Luca, a one star increase in Yelp rating is equivalent to a five to nine percent increase in revenue.[23] As such, the stakes are high and incentive high enough for fake reviews. In fact, there is accumulating evidence on the gaming of review sites.[24] Companies, such as Klout, are stepping into this niche in order to provide some balance.

Quantity matters, but so does quality. While quantity is a surrogate in many cases for quality, as Google's history as a search engine has shown, we still need other checks and balances for quality in social media content. For example, a company that sells eyeglasses online got to the top of Google rankings because of all the negative remarks about it. It kept selling more because of its ranking, and kept getting more negative comments, that continued keeping it at the top of Google rankings. The owner of the site continued exploiting this cause and effect relationship since it was beneficial.[25] When the New York Times reported the story, Google responded by admitting that it needed to consider sentiment analysis in its search ranking algorithm.[26]

Another example is that of Yelp reviews which although true do not reflect the views of your primary target market. According to Professor Duncan Simester, the views of younger clientele who were not their primary target market skewed the reviews of his restaurant on Yelp. This younger audience with more time to write online reviews complained about unreasonable prices of higher quality sandwiches that the restaurant's primary target audience of older clientele was quite happy to pay for.[27]

Such incidents reveal the weaknesses of measuring popularity and usefulness of online content based on quantity measures alone. This could make an open but administered approach to community content generation, such as ones from Quora and Wikipedia take on more importance for many companies as well. Wikipedia members step in to correct any errors and any content generated is, by open admission, considered work in progress. Quora, although not as large in scale as Wikipedia, allows its users to edit questions, upvote answers, and has a well-stated policy to create and maintain expectations on what is desirable behavior and appropriate content for its site.

Chapter 6 Summary and Key Takeaways

■ Build trust through open communication on social networks. In some ways, likes, tweets, and shares have become a representation of trust to other customers and prospects.

■ While the number of likes and shares might represent an endorsement and trust, it is not the same as taste. Thus, you still need ways to connect prospects with other prospects who are unknown to them but have similar taste.

■ The proliferation of information on social networks has led to an increase in quantity, which makes it difficult to gauge quality. This could make an open but administered approach to community building such as Quora and Wikipedia take on more importance. Quora, for example, sets expectations upfront on what is an acceptable response.

Chapter 7

Return on Investment

Nobody knows anything and nobody cares. Being on the leading front of marketing liberates you from accountability...
—*Anon*

What is a "Like" Worth?

All companies are trying to invest in customer engagement. We measure this engagement in terms of likes, tweets, shares, and comments; however, nobody knows their worth except for "positive hope." Is a fan more likely to buy? As a recent *PC World* article suggested, the race in social media seems to be about acquiring more followers, more tweets, more re-tweets and so on without regard to what exactly they translate into in terms of bottom line to the business.[1]

Joe Fernandez, founder of Klout, says that, for the first time, word of mouth has become scalable and measurable, which is how the idea for measuring influence sprouted as a Klout Score.[2] Word of mouth has always been invisible but valuable. It has also been unmeasurable and unscalable. The ability to measure and scale it is a tremendous asset; however, only the measurement is in the company's control. Scaling it is in the hands of the customer with the company acting as a positive or a negative catalyst.

As Klout's chief executive officer (CEO) Joe Fernandez explains, no one is in a hurry to spend too much on social media when it is hard to show results.[3] Social media is yet to correlate in most cases with direct sales; however, it appears to be successful, whenever combined with a contest or coupon.

Most companies are still using their experimental marketing budget and still turning to search engines as the place for advertising that is closer to a sale. In other words, for most companies today, social media is experimental and hip, but they are not allocating too much resource to it.

What is a "Fan" Worth?

Fans could like your updates frequently (or not so frequently). In other words, fans may be at varying levels of engagement. Therefore, it becomes hard to calculate the exact worth of a fan. If they became fans just to get a coupon or discount, they obviously have cost the company the face value of the coupon.

In a study by SocialCode, the estimated worth of a fan was $9.56, assuming a constant cost of a dollar per click and dividing that by the total number of actions performed.[4] The actions they looked at were both purchase and nonpurchase related, such as contest participation.

There are different ways of looking at how much a fan is worth. For example, it costs $1.07 to advertise on Facebook to encourage a user to become a fan;[5] however, these "fans" may already be buying and are committed buyers of your brand. Fandom provides a place where you can continue to engage regularly with your fans, which is the true value of acquiring a fan base. Another study calculated the average value of a fan as $136.38, based on how much they spent, how much more loyal they were, how much they recommended the brand to others, and how much they saved in acquisition cost.[6]

Although the dollar amount placed on the worth of a fan might be different, one common thing comes across: These fans are your most engaged customers, whether through participating in contests, paying more visits to your Website, or spending more on your product compared to nonfans.

The interesting statistic here, though, is not that fans are spending more across all companies examined. The interesting question to ask is, "Why is an Oreo® fan spending only $28.52 more than a nonfan, while a McDonald's fan is spending $159.79 more than a nonfan?"[7] Could Oreo be doing better by having a better strategy? In other words, what you get out of your fans depends on the effectiveness of your strategy.

According to Clearspring, the company that makes the well-known Website tool AddThis®, LinkedIn does not drive as much traffic as Twitter or Facebook, but LinkedIn drives 1.5 clicks per article shared compared to an average of 1.1 across all networks.[8] LinkedIn is more effective for generating leads for business-to-business (B2B).

The return on investment (ROI) you receive depends a lot on how you structure your message and whether your business objective, your intended target audience, and your message are in alignment. As said earlier, each social network provides different strengths and weaknesses. Facebook, for example, provides a great amount of granularity in terms of information on your target market that it becomes very attractive; however, most Facebook users are not on the network paying attention to its ads.[9] In terms of granularity of information, what Facebook provides is lost as an advantage to marketers because of people's lack of focus and intent on its advertisements.

Unlike Google users, most Facebook users are not going there with the intention to search for product information. That is true for many social networks. This might change as their search functions get better; however, the fact is that today, each social network has carved out its own niche, serving a different aspect of benefits of a social network.

Social Media Is Not Free

We may not know exactly what a "like" or a "tweet" is worth, but we do know that, despite the seemingly free nature of social media, it is not free.[10] It requires consistent, daily dedication, and a small but dedicated amount of time to provide updates, gauge the general nature of comments, and understand your audience and the success of your updates. Due to the fragmented nature of social media, you need to give this small but dedicated amount of time to all social networks that matter to your company. Thus, any company has to choose from the start the ones that make the most sense strategically, depending on customers and objectives.

One reason that social media has become popular as a communication channel for companies is its low barriers to entry and popularity among target customers. Once entered, it requires an investment of intellectual energy with consistency at short intervals. Unlike other channels of communication, such as weekly or fortnightly email campaigns, social media requires a consistent feed of thought at least twice a day (if not more) to cross the threshold of effectiveness due to more noise.

Although this does not seem like a lot, the fragmentation of audiences and different demographics on different social networks multiply the need for this effort. In some ways, it is similar to the way email was once—free. Yet, email has turned out to require management, messaging, analysis of metrics for fine-tuning, follow-up response, and an effort at greater efficacy and ROI. Email has also turned into phishing and scam messaging that misrepresent companies. As a result, it has resulted in a need for monitoring and flagging to protect customers.

Many companies are entering the social Web but without investments. It seems like a cool thing to do and perceived as forward thinking in your marketing efforts. In most cases, the budget is pulled out of the experimental side of marketing. Social is free to enter but costs to maintain and monitor.

It is free since there are no costs in creating a Facebook, Twitter, or LinkedIn account. It is expensive (measured in amount of time spent) because anyone can do so and that creates more competition for attention. The barriers to entry for getting into social media are seemingly none; however, once you get in to grow it, monitor it, track it, and manage it, your efforts begin, which can become expensive.

When used as a channel of communication, social media has a cost of ownership due to required maintenance, monitoring, tracking, and management, whether or not you created it. Its low barriers to entry can lead to unabandoned proliferation, which suggests the need for a corporate-wide strategy for social media with a budget that recognizes its total cost of ownership. Anyone—a fan, an employee, or a competitor— can create a company page. Such unmanaged proliferation is a challenge since you cannot measure what you do not know.

You may not want to keep going once you have started, which calls for a strategy to unwind in a gracious manner without alienating your fans and followers.

Part of the problem with the approach or lack of a strategic approach by companies to social media is that it is nothing but word of mouth in an online medium. You cannot manipulate word of mouth, but it has always been happening. If you look at the different channels through which your customers come to you, you can always attribute some to customer, co-worker, and friend referrals. Others come through channels such as email campaigns, sales, and advertising. While your ROI is clear on the other channels, you will never attempt to create a budget to get customers actively through word of mouth. Today, social media is a tool through which you can actively seek or enhance word of mouth while giving you a chance to measure it.

In his book, *Social Media ROI*, Oliver Blanchard speaks of the two questions that often come up when broaching the use of social media with business executives. The first is, "Why should we use it.? If our customers are not using it, why should we? I don't use it myself, so why should I expect my customers to be using it?"[11] This confusion arises from the fact that we have clubbed all social media together.

The best analogy to relate to this confusion is to ask the question, "Why should we advertise on television, radio, or print?" Similarly, social media refers to a set of different media in which communication is, by its nature, interactive or has the potential to be interactive. You advertise on television if you think your audience is watching television. You advertise on specific programs or channels that your specific target market prefers. Social media is no different. As shown in earlier chapters on demographics and usage,[12] different groups use different networks for different purposes and at different levels of usage. The appropriate question to ask would be, "Which of the social media channels is my target customer likely to use?"

According to Blanchard, a second question, laden with fear, that often comes up is "What if we do not hear anything good or customers say negative things?"[13] This fear is about managing a crisis or a general sense that there are things that need fixing. You could use this as an opportunity to find out. Using social media tools, why not ask customers directly about ways to improve? This is more of an issue for a company with an already built brand reputation. If so, this might be a chance to sustain and strengthen your brand instead of letting it erode.

Is Fear Keeping You Away?

Companies can do several things if this fear is keeping them away from social media. Are there inherent weaknesses that you fear will come out in the open? If there are some specific negative issues, they might already be out there on the social Web as a Yelp or Amazon review or on some other forum. You might want to fix it before initiating a social conversation, or you could start out by making the social conversation part of the process.

If the fear stems from legal issues, then any involvement requires legal counsel from the beginning. If the fear stems from giving employees too much freedom or losing control over presenting a uniform image to the outside world, then you need to constantly remind, train, and inform your employees about social media policy by setting specific guidelines. It is also important that the company culture be worthy of its brand reputation.

Most companies do not set out to use social media by tying it to specific business objectives. Instead, they tie social media initiatives to vague goals, disconnected from business objectives (e.g., "our competitors have a Facebook page, so we should too" or "I don't know what social media will do for us, but let's test the waters"). Some social media users say it is immeasurable but nonetheless important to do; others do it without specific objectives.

Social media is for building relationships. Today, those relationships may not be directly worthwhile. As Bibb and Kourdy's book on trust says, many executives know or feel sure that there is a positive relationship between "culture of trust" and profitability of a company;[14] however, like many important and hard-to-measure concepts such as happiness, creativity, and love, it remains a nebulous concept.

Some social media users feel the same way; however, it is possible that some of them have jumped into social media without objectives that tie to business performance. For example, if you measure your success in social media by the number of "likes" or "followers," how much does it affect your bottom line? Are they prospects or current customers? Are they advocates and users of your products? Like the concept of trust building, is it possible that some of these followers, who are not existing customers, could potentially become customers or introduce you to potential prospects down the road? Thus, although it is difficult to measure accurately, it is not impossible to track.

Measuring ROI for social media need not be any different from measuring ROI in other areas if you tie use of the tools to business objectives. Many software programs measure different things, and what you need depends on what specific key performance indicators you think are valuable and best tied to your business objectives. Increasing the number of fans or followers is a good objective. However, did that result in an increase in sales to your customers?

The best way to look at how successful these tools are is to compare them with word of mouth. Before the age of social media tools, you would not have known exactly what other readers were thinking about any published article, except through selectively published letters to the editor in some cases. For any major news article published today, you can see by the number of tweets and shares how often it is shared and, by looking at the content and sentiment of the tweets, whether it was positively received. This would not have been possible before the age of transparent digital sharing. The other positive aspect of the tools today is the amplified word of mouth that allows for distributing the article so quickly among so many. That is the power of social media. The risk is the transparency that it brings to this process of social communication, which could backfire when it is negative.

A comparison between traditional media and digital media might bring more clarity here. Traditionally, as the saying goes, you know you are wasting half the dollars you spent on television advertising—you just did not know which half! Effectiveness, as measured by direct sales or other research-based attitude and awareness numbers, were the only ways to measure. These were done by an external agency, such as through Nielsen ratings, that was not necessarily perfect but as good as it got. Radio and print advertising were similar with no feedback unless you included a call to action, such as a coupon or a short-term offer.

Search engine advertising changed the rules in the traditional media world by letting you reach buyers at the time they were considering a purchase. Moreover, a new type of skill (e.g., figuring out the best keywords to use) was required. It was also within the reach of any company. You did not need a multimillion-dollar budget anymore.

Facebook advertising is somewhat similar to search engine advertising (See Figure 7.1) except that they gear it towards refined targeting based on psychographics, and not necessarily at the time of purchase. You gear social media toward sharing and exponentially growing your reach. In this case, the challenge is to provide something of informational or entertainment value, and the focus is on building trust—one share at a time.

Figure 7.1: Differences among Communication Channels

Channel	Creative Effort	Targeting	Cost of Entry	Feedback
Television	High	Interest	High	Indirect
Radio	Medium	Interest	Medium	Indirect
Print	Medium	Interest	Medium	Indirect
Search engine ads	Low	Keyword	Low	Direct
Facebook	Low High	Demographics and Interests	Low	Direct
Twitter	Low	Keywords	Low	Direct
LinkedIn	Low	Occupation and Skills	Low	Direct

Facebook has struggled while trying to figure out how to make its advertising more effective. It is similar to how search engines took some time to figure out that the best advertisements do not pop up but relate instead to keywords typed by users. Since they are looking for something related to that keyword, advertisements based on keywords became a huge success.

Mark Zuckerberg had similar thoughts when he spoke to his current vice present of marketing, David Fischer, about how he envisioned advertising on Facebook to be unlike any before. In January 2011, Fischer, operating on that philosophy, launched "sponsored stories," for which advertisers have to pay, allowing advertisers to highlight status updates or "likes" related to their brands as sponsored stories.[15]

Starting 2012, Facebook started delivery of these sponsored stories as "newsfeed" instead of appearing on the sides as display ads. Facebook individuals connect, on average, to 130 people, each of whom connects on average with 130 each, separated by four degrees of freedom.[16] Such "social endorsement ads" could prove more powerful for Facebook and its advertisers than ordinary display ads if combined with other psychographical data that is Facebook's greatest value.

Facebook's "like" button, representing an emotional sensor, has turned out to be quite valuable.[17] Proctor & Gamble CEO Robert McDonald says that things like Facebook and Google can be much more efficient, which should also probably push televisions into the Internet realm more quickly.[18] The company is trimming its $10 billion advertising budget, looking for productive innovation in advertising, which the new media represent.

While search engine advertising has proven to be popular with all business to consumer (B2C) and B2B companies, Facebook's treasure trove of personal information, including voluntary endorsements of products and services that people seem willing to share, is a different type of asset for companies. Facebook is limited, however, to the B2C space, with LinkedIn geared toward B2B customers and Twitter toward both B2C and B2B customers as social spheres for conversations.

An analysis of tweets on Twitter over 223 days shows that Twitter is still mostly a distribution vehicle for information.[19] The difference is that there are more individuals now doing it as opposed to, for example, unpersonalized media. In addition, it includes bloggers who comprise a significant proportion of those tweeters. Just as the theory of communication that first introduced the notion of opinion leaders would suggest, a small portion of mostly celebrities, organizations, media people, and bloggers dominate half of all communication; the other 50% are ordinary users, defined as not having too many followers.[20]

There is also a two-step format where information shared is often re-tweeted; at other times, independent discovery by another tweeter leads to its re-introduction. Another significant finding by the researchers was that, although bloggers seem to introduce information from media and organizations, for the greater proportion of these four groups, there is more homophily with celebrities paying more attention to other celebrities, and with media paying more attention to other media.[21]

The bottom line is that, in terms of ROI, much depends on building your followership if you are not one of the elite, as defined by the researchers as having many followers (i.e., over 5,000).[22] Another aspect of how information flows on Twitter is the way in which intermediaries (i.e., those with 543 followers on average) seem to influence ordinary users. Intermediaries seem more connected with media and serve as a conduit for a two-step information flow.

What is the Return on Investment in Social Media?

There are a couple of flaws when asking this question. Using social media successfully takes time and effort, which translates into cost. Many marketers have got into social media without any allocated resources and without any clear business objectives. Most are spending less than $10,000 and allocating three or fewer employees; 40% are spending one to five hours on social media marketing per week.[23]

The point of using social media is for building and nurturing customer relationships. No other venue gives you the opportunity to interact directly with customers and get feedback. You receive immediate feedback on how much people share something you post or publish, as well as a comparison to other posts and published work to gauge your "influence." Without in-built sharing, it is impossible for you to get that type of feedback from traditional print, radio, or television.

However, to get people to share, you first need to build an audience. When you use an already established community, the first step (i.e., establishing a following) takes care of itself to some extent. To that end, you need to say the right things to attract the kind of audience you want. If you are an established brand, it is a little easier because people already know your name.

For example, Whole Foods Market's objective is to attract an audience interested in wholesome, organic, nutritious, and higher priced food that people are willing to pay for. Their first objective is to establish an online following of a target market interested in this message. Social media is not for promoting directly and shamelessly. Instead, you have to build an audience that is willing to pay you with social media currency … and more.

Social Media Return on Investment in Time

BUILD LISTENING SKILLS

You cannot measure social media ROI immediately; it takes time. The first step to building your social media asset is listening. It is not surprising that the term used for monitoring social media conversations is "listening." You listen to what customers and prospects, or any audience you want to monitor, are saying. Of the many available listening tools, only some are free.

Once you have listened, you need to do a number of things, such as look for patterns and summarize what those patterns possibly mean. For example, Stern's Center for Measurable Marketing at New York University used a paid tool called Crimson Hexagon to capture all of the social media conversations. By drilling down, they could put the conversations in three buckets:

1. Conversations around purchase behavior
2. Conversations around the company's media and marketing activities

3. General emotions expressed toward the brand, such as how much they loved the brand or store

According to the director of Stern's Center, Craig Stacey, looking at levels of conversation or sentiment is not as good a predictor as general emotion toward the brand or store.[24]

Ultimately, a human has to make sense of and analyze everything said. Although we call these "listening" tools, they are just search tools that help you capture everything, or the most relevant conversations and news on the social Web that is now the Internet.

One way to listen is to be proactive and use a tool, such as Google Alerts, to set up the topics, brands, or keywords on which you would like to stay informed. Google then sends regular emails with a collection of news articles mentioning the keywords you have chosen. Twitter Search is another tool, better now than before, which looks at the streams of tweets related to a keyword.

A third tool is Technorati, which is a blog search engine. There are also specialized search engines focusing on social media conversations only, such as socialmention, that gathers all the tweets and Facebook mentions related to a keyword.

Some of the paid tools present all of the information as a dashboard and provide analytics, such as how many "likes" you have had on Facebook over time. Using just one tool does not help since each tool does some things better than others; however, using a number of tools together starts painting a good overview of how your brand is perceived, how you can use the information for your marketing activities, and who are the strongest likely influencers.

Figure 7.2 shows a snapshot of search results on "Chobani yogurt" with two different social media monitoring tools.

Figure 7.2: Snapshot of Search Results in socialmention and Topsy™

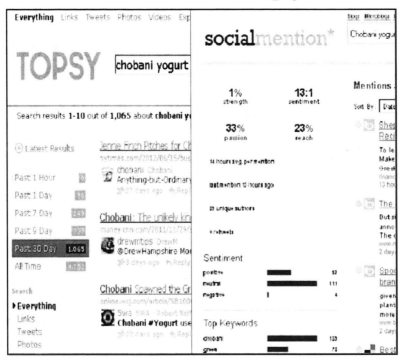

Topsy™ shows mentions and a basic analysis but does not provide sentiment analysis. On the other hand, socialmention provides for sentiment analysis as well. These tools are acceptable for monitoring and free; however, for deeper investigation, other advanced tools are available that require greater expertise in statistics, which is beyond the scope of this book.

BUILD AN AUDIENCE

The second step in building your social media asset is to build an audience you can communicate "with" —not "at." To that end, you have to think about what you can provide that will be of value, so they will gather around you (metaphorically speaking).

Former National Basketball Association player Shaquille O'Neal measures his Twitter success by the number of followers. He says that 60% of his tweets are inspirational, 30% are humorous, and the balance is sales.[25] Thus, you need to provide something of value to build an audience. Once you have an audience, you need social media currency.

BUILD SOCIAL MEDIA CURRENCY

The third step to getting a valuable ROI from social media is to build social media currency. Social media currency is the new currency of the Web. It is highly valuable because it gives you permission to communicate with your potential target market.

According to a recent survey, even though online ad spending is going up, consumers are fed up with intrusive digital advertising;[26] however, the same consumers liked ads relating to personal interests (e.g., contextual or location-specific). In such an environment, establishing an audience that is giving you permission to speak to them through new variations of social currency is valuable. We measure this social currency through "likes," "shares," "tweets," or "pins," to name a few.

Giving your prospects access to the many ways of sharing extends your potential reach, although some forms of currency stay more valuable, depending on where you will find your target market or which of the social channels is the most preferred by your target market.

AUDIENCE: THE REAL ASSET IN SOCIAL MEDIA

When your target market gives you permission to speak to them through social media currency, you can turn this opportunity into something more valuable when they respond in a positive way. They will tell more people about you, re-tweet what you have said or done, or share something you have shared with them with their circles. This is likely to result in more people becoming part of your permission-based audience. After all, in an era of fragmenting channels, when attention is a limited resource, is not getting an audience that has given you permission to communicate with them a valuable asset?

The new social media networks are giving you the ability to communicate with your audience with their permission—now called "earned media" as opposed to "paid media." Earned media, such as articles published by reporters with product mention, have always held more sway for consumers compared to paid media. Today, however, these earnings are coming from all kinds of places, such as bloggers and ordinary consumers talking to each other. Now, when consumers talk on line, companies have an opportunity to listen in; if they are proactive, they can actually weigh in.

Marketing on these social networks cannot be blatant. It needs to be preceded by providing something of value while building a name and brand personality indirectly. This is what the new age of social Web calls for: subtle marketing to an audience that has given you permission to speak to them and that will reward you with more social media currency as well as real currency if things are done right.

Whole Foods Market has been using Pinterest to create 22 boards with issues relevant to its customers, who do not buy only for "organic" reasons. They buy because they are interested in local issues, recycling, and sustainability, or they care about the community. Whole Foods Market has only 15,000 followers for its brand but over 22,000 followers for some of the boards created around the core values of its brand. Some of its recipes have been repinned on other boards. On none of these boards does Whole Foods Market promote itself blatantly.[27]

This has become the hallmark of social media. All promotion is understated and limited, and happens after offering something of value. Whole Foods Market has seen a traffic increase to its Website from Pinterest, and more coming from images of recipes and positive recommendations posted for those recipes.[28]

According to Michael Bepko, Global Community Manager for Whole Foods Market, at this time, there is no way to calculate the ROI in terms of purchase at the checkout.[29] Regardless, it is driving traffic to its Website and presents many prospects and customers that have given it permission to communicate with them. This is a brick-and-mortar store. For an online store, the ROI should be easier to measure.

BOTTOM LINE

If you do the above steps right and consistently, it is likely to result in a positive feedback loop with your permission-based audience having greater awareness of your brand. When it is time for purchase, you are likely to get serious consideration. If you deliver on their expectations and more, you are likely to hear about it through the channels you have already established. This gives you the chance to strengthen the relationship you have worked hard to establish and nurture. Thus, social media ROI is a process that needs time and fine-tuning with the additional benefit of revealing weaknesses that have gone unnoticed or are hidden well due to lack of transparency.

If you feel that your company has things to fix, it might be a good time to do so because social media is for those who want honest customer interaction. One of the reasons companies are hesitant to jump into social media is fear. That fear, although unnamed, is what your customer is going to say. If that is holding you back, you might want to find out what your customers think through other means, fix what needs fixing, and then launch your social interactions.

Given that the benefits of building a social media asset should be clear, the question is how much to spend on it.

Social Media Spending

Views on social media spending are changing. Most marketers expect spending on digital media to go up significantly, with social media accounting for 27% of the digital media budget in 2012.[30] The trends are clear. Marketing budgets need to follow prospects and customers.

According to *eMarketer*, U.S. adults are spending more time online with time on the Internet growing 6% a year. The biggest losers are traditional print newspapers and magazines. Television and video, while still maintaining a large share of the amount of time spent, are declining albeit slowly. As of 2010, U.S. adults spent an average of four hours and 24 minutes each day watching television and video compared to two hours and 34 minutes online.[31] At this rate, time spent on the Internet will be as much as time spent on the television by 2015, if not more.

The best way to look at the transition from traditional to digital and social is to follow consumer time on different channels and advertising spending, which understandably lags user behavior. According to the Internet Advertising Bureau, Internet advertising spending has increased 22% on a yearly basis to $7.9 billion in the third quarter of 2011.[32] In contrast, television advertising, which is still big, drew $60.7 billion in 2011 (annual) according to *eMarketer* estimates.[33]

This compares with $2.02 billion on online video spending. Although small by comparison, online video advertising grew 55% from 2010.[34] More than 100 million Americans watched online video on an average day. This is also growing, showing a 43% year-over-year increase.[35] Online media giants have noticed the importance of attracting advertisers to the digital space. For example, Google, Yahoo, Microsoft, and AOL® are planning a 2012 event in New York, highlighting their upcoming programming to attract more advertising dollars.

However, to put things in perspective, while a typical U.S. adult spends on average four hours and 24 minutes on television per day[36] (The Bureau of Labor Statistics puts this figure closer to three hours a day),[37] the amount of daily time spent on Facebook is about 10 to 15 minutes on average.[38] Thus, the amount of time spent on the Internet is growing. However, users divide their time on the Internet among many different channels (Websites), and the holding time per channel is a lot less than it is on television. However, because it targets better, and because the consumer is spending time on that particular channel by intention (as in search) or by permission (as in social media), the chance of getting their attention is higher.

As the lines between online video and television video begin to blur with penetration of smart televisions, the necessity of comparing time spent on traditional television and on the Internet begins to blur as well. Targeted video advertising becomes more powerful.

As new televisions, which integrate with the Internet, arrive in the marketplace and penetrate households, the Internet takes on more significance. Consumers are shifting many activities they did offline (e.g., reading books and newspapers, watching movies, communicating, and now socializing) to the online medium. The dollars spent on marketing need to shift accordingly.

As is evident from the *Forrester* forecast, U.S. spending on interactive media as of 2011 was $ 34.3 billion, and expectations cite up to $77 billion by 2016. In terms of trends, search, social, email, online display ads (including display ads on social media channels), and mobile advertising will continue to grow. These come at the expense of traditional media spending.[39]

As spending on social media grows, we will start seeing allocation by type of social channel, including spending on tools, services, and building of social assets. Search engine advertising still carries certain benefits, such as the customer starting the search process with a keyword. As search engines within social channels improve, it could change to a focus on intentional search in a social context. Google is already deploying Google+ recommendations in its search results.

Although Twitter search function is reasonably good in this regard, most social networks are not very good in their search capabilities. Currently though, social channels provide the advantage of discovery through trusted sources (i.e., other customers, greater reach through sharing, increased awareness, and the ability to build on customer audiences as a social media asset, with which you can then communicate on a regular basis).

Figure 7.3: Percentage Budget Allocation by Media in 2011

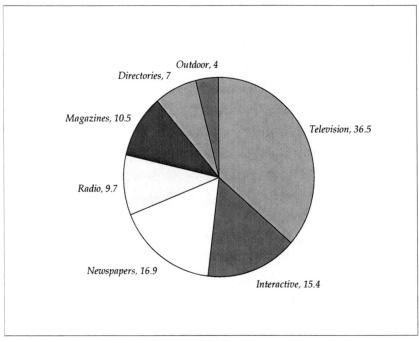

Source: eMarketer.com

Figure 7.4: Expected Percentage Budget Allocation by Media in 2015

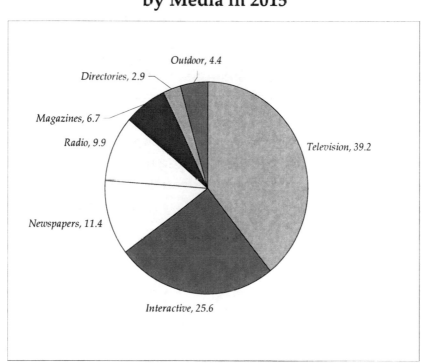

Source: eMarketer.com

Trends are very clear. As shown in Figures 7.3 and 7.4,[40] U.S. television advertising represented 36.5 % of a total estimated advertising budget of $144 billion[41] in 2011. While the total pie may grow in keeping with the economy, it is clear that the share of budget allocated to interactive media will grow from 15.4% in 2011 to 25.6% in 2015.

The major losers are print magazines, directories, and radio. The major gainers will be, in general, interactive advertising, particularly social media channels; mobile; all forms of more targeted, online display advertising; and online video advertisements. Search and email will continue to grow; however, they will compete with other online advertising formats, such as contextual display, video, and social media.

Proctor & Gamble, the consumer products giant, aims to save $10 billion by 2016 by cutting $1 billion from its advertising budget.[42] Its goal is to rely heavily on lower cost digital marketing at the expense of higher cost broadcast advertising. Its chief of global marketing, Marc Pritchard, is working with the National Association of Advertising to develop an electronic gross rating point (GRP) standard, which could be used similarly to the traditional GRP system for traditional media.

EVOLUTION OF EMAIL

It is hard to think of the time when there was no email when you are constantly under bombardment by it. Yet, it is also hard to think of a modern world without email despite the volume of spam. It is still how many of us communicate for business and even for personal purposes. Social media for communication has its place but for a different purpose — perhaps for connecting with friends and keeping them updated without expecting (at least not explicitly) a return response, almost like an "FYI."

Email, on the other hand, is for greater accountability and tracking. It is not for collaboration whereas you could design social media that way. This explains how and why email is available with Facebook, yet only a few use it. This also explains why Facebook continues to send billions of emails a day to its users, urging them to go back and check for updates, as do other social networks. Thus, social networks have not replaced your regular email, such as Google's Gmail or Yahoo! Mail as a communication tool.

If anything, email programs are beginning to leverage the advantages of social media by adding the ability to share. Companies like CalmSea, Inc., have started leveraging social data to develop more targeted emails that seem to increase response rate by 50%.[43]

While personalization of email has always been the Holy Grail, it failed to achieve its goals because you could lie about your age or your interests for privacy reasons. Social networks, on the other hand, force people to be relatively honest about themselves, their likes, and their interests. In addition, as interests continue to evolve, there is an opportunity to capture these changes automatically through social network applications. According to CalmSea, Inc., with Facebook Connect, the company has seen 70% opt-in for sharing of social data through the apps the company has developed for its clients.[44]

Email marketing has definitely had an impact on direct mail. It is capable of targeting with precision, and it tells you whether the intended recipient opened it. It gives you the ability to get a response, if any, and in whatever degree quickly. Email marketing has mostly replaced direct mail, but it has not abolished it; it has added another touchpoint.

Social media marketing is no different. It provides certain advantages. It is going to be another component that is already taking away dollars from traditional forms of television, radio, and print advertising; however, since the barriers to entry into social media allow anyone to use it, rising above the noise could give television advertising an edge with its higher barriers to entry in terms of cost.

Does Print Have a Place?

All forms of print are seeing a decline while time spent online continues to increase. Newspaper circulation is down, on average (8.7% annually), which is also reflected in their revenues. For every $1 gained in digital revenues, newspapers are losing $7 in print revenue.[45] As of February 2012, almost half (46%) of Americans owned a smartphone. As of January 2012, 29% of U.S. adults owned either an e-reader or a tablet device.[46] In December 2011, e-books were the most popular format for the top 42 of 50 top-selling titles listed in *USA Today*.[47]

In 2012, we see the official turning point for print as *Encyclopedia Britannica* finally stopped its print edition, which has not been its main revenue generator for a while. As consumers turn more to digital media for information and entertainment, advertising dollars will also follow them. Print is not likely to disappear. It will continue to have a place for generating attention, as the digital space gets more crowded. With print on demand, printing costs are going down significantly as well.

Chapter 7 Summary and Key Takeaways

■ Each social network brings certain strengths and weaknesses. The ROI you receive depends on how you structure your message, and whether your message aligns with your intended target audience and your business objective.

■ Use social media to build and nurture customer relationships. No other venue gives you the opportunity to interact directly with customers and get feedback.

■ You need to measure the ROI in social media over time using different metrics. The focus initially needs to be in building an asset of audience that is giving you permission to speak to them in an age of information deluge and attention deficit.

■ Social media marketing will continue to grow, even as email adds social elements and uses social data to become effective, and televisions become smarter and more integrated with the Internet.

Chapter 8

Role of Websites in a Social Web

It is NOT location, location, location!

It is keyword, keyword, and keyword!

Your Website Is Still Important

In traditional marketing, success has always been about location, location, location! In today's world of digitally connected consumers—who, more often than not, start their consumer journey online—marketing is about keyword, keyword, keyword!

Keywords are the precious and valuable words that customers and prospects use to find their way to your Website. They could use these words to conduct a search on Twitter, known as a "hashtag" (keywords preceded by the # symbol). All social networks have come up with their own nomenclature to denote similar yet different terms.

When writing on your Website, it is very important to use keywords your customers and prospects will choose. A fully developed ecosystem about using appropriate keywords and enriching your Website copy with those keywords now exists. Think about your audience when you tweet, and include appropriate hashtags that will help them find you through Twitter to your Website.

Websites are still as important in your marketing strategy as they were in early 2000. Recently, companies like Facebook have been trying to woo prospects into building full-fledged stores using their platform.[1] Investing too much in a secondary social network platform carries several risks. Many social network platforms exist, and each is attractive to different demographic groups for different reasons. To put all your eggs into one basket, or to invest too much in one to the exclusion of the other, is a mistake.

Clearly, this is a fast-changing area. Although social networks are here to stay, and represent the traditional word-of-mouth communication taking a different format, the technology underlying a particular social network will continue to change. The one thing over which you have control is your Website, which is where you should direct your customer traffic as much as possible.

There are other reasons why directing traffic to your Website is advantageous. The strength of your digital media strategy now comes from three areas:

1. Being discovered through social networks and search engines
2. Being spoken about in a positive way
3. Persuading others through the content on your Website

When people discover you through social networks, it becomes more complicated due to fragmentation of all those channels. The more people you can bring to your Website, the more opportunities you have to build an ongoing relationship with your prospects and customers through email. People still check email far more than social networks for significant daily communication.

Social media, search engines, and your Website interact in several ways. To the extent that your site's content is easy to share, it increases your reach. Any current Website needs to provide the tools to share content. This means that you also need to provide something of value that people want to share, such as:

■ Information-rich content and coupons
■ Sharable features, such as images that can be pinned
■ Videos that are likely to be shared on Facebook
■ Whitepapers that are likely to be distributed through Twitter or shared through LinkedIn

Since you can share content through multiple channels in tiers, any way you can implicitly reference your original site is an opportunity to win customer share of mind.

Many companies, such as Zynga, started out using a social network as the primary platform. Some have pulled away to reduce their dependence on the social network and develop their own Website. As the number of networks multiply, it becomes more obvious that reliance solely on any one is a business risk.

Your Website—particularly a mobile (e.g., mobile phone and tablet friendly) Website—will continue to be important to reduce reliance on any particular platform. Facebook designed its new timeline feature to give companies a chance to replace their Website content by providing a more graphical and storytelling format for your interface. It also wanted to encourage companies to advertise more on Facebook by reducing the direct feeds from companies to their fans. While these changes might make the Facebook company page more attractive, it would still be a mistake to rely on it to the exclusion of a corporate Website.

Given the number of different social networks, and the very different reasons for use and demographics on each, relying on a single social network is obviously not the answer for reaching your audience.

Chapter 8 Summary and Key Takeaways

■ In a world of digital marketing, you can determine success by keyword, keyword, and keyword! and not location, location, location!

■ Social networks are fragmented and continue to change. Hence, your Website is still important. Websites provide you with control as you continue to build social elements into your site.

Chapter 9

Role of Search Engines in a Social Web

Search and social are on a collision course. Google is adding social capabilities and other tools are making it easier to search for and discover social conversations.

History of Search

Parallels can be drawn between the emergence of the Web and the creation of so many Websites that were first manually collected by search engines, yet most of the famous search engines of those days (e.g., Lycos® and Excite®) could not keep up with the pace of information creation. Google came up with a much better algorithm that could figure out the most relevant results based on what other users thought. In some ways, Google used crowdsourcing in its algorithms to determine what was most relevant. Search engines were supposed to make it easier for people to find relevant information, yet even they could not keep up.

We now have a similar issue with content created on social networks usually closed to search engines. Most of these social networks, used by different groups for different purposes, have an inferior search interface. To put it simply, search is not their forte except for Google, which has its own social network (Google+).

A cursory search for a few major companies, on a single social network such as Facebook, shows the difficulty of knowing and managing your organization's social media presence. A random, small sample of companies shows that they have multiple Facebook pages, sometimes created by the same groups (presumably unbeknownst to each other); other times, different groups create them and occasionally use different logos (see Figure 9.1).

Figure 9.1: Manual Search Results on Company Facebook Pages

Company	Number of Facebook Pages	Types of Pages
Apple Inc.	Greater than 10	Corporate, product specific, country specific, store, unofficial (by users/fans), Wikipedia®
Ford®	Greater than 10	Ford (4 different pages), Ford product or model specific such as Ford Mustang, Ford trucks, usage (Ford racing), country-specific (Ford Mexico)
Dell™	Greater than 10	Dell (at least two different pages), Dell Spot (Canadian/customer support), Dell Enterprise, Dell country specific pages (e.g. Dell Vietnam), Dell Deals page, Dell Lounge (another promotional page), social media for business page (to discuss business-to-business use of social media)

Source: SMStrat (http://www.smstrat.com)

For example, there are multiple Ford® Facebook pages (i.e., one for corporate; some product specific; some created by fans; and sometimes for the same purpose, such as for products and services but obviously created by two different groups or individuals from the same corporation). While social media is supposed to be natural and organic, such unabandoned and unmonitored growth of your social media corporate presence is cumbersome at the very least, and a threat to branding, corporate strategy, and security at the other extreme.

As Figure 9.1 illustrates, discovering your current social presence is unmanageable when done manually; however, using tools (e.g., SocialiQ Network's platform) for social presence discovery makes it a lot easier to find a starting benchmark for management and control of social media channels.

It is clear from Figure 9.2 that, using SocialiQ Network's discovery platform, the search for "Apple computers" shows its greatest presence on Facebook in terms of number of pages and its presence on other networks. The technology provides other options to drill down further; therefore, depending on departmental functions and the engagement level on each of the social surfaces, anyone could choose to monitor, track, manage, or request deletion of any one of these social pages, groups, or profiles.

It is obvious from Figure 9.2 that you cannot manually manage or monitor all of the social conversations taking place in the social Web. This is similar to what happened with search engines, which started as a manually selected listing of all information on the Web as Yahoo!; however, as the Web grew, it was even impossible for Yahoo! to keep up and make it easier to find information. Today, we need the tools to discover relevant social spaces at the macro level. That is what SocialiQ Networks does as a discovery engine.

Figure 9.2: Social Presence of Apple Inc.

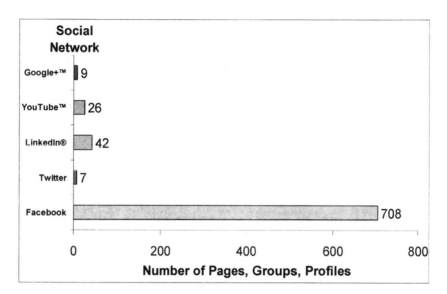

Source: http://www.socialiqnetworks.com/

A latecomer dominating as the leading search engine, Google is again a latecomer in the social network arena. Some of the recent announcements by Google to include social network results on the search pages do two things:

1. It makes Google+ social conversations more readily available to Google than Facebook and Twitter, putting other social networks at a disadvantage.
2. Having a Google+ profile on Google would be an advantage, which could essentially force the other social networks to open up more in order not to lose their audience to Google+.

One of the recent announcements from Google[1] about its personal results means that social media activity is going to count toward results related to the keywords that go into your digital marketing materials. Google and other search engines are beginning to take into account a number of factors in bringing up results from social conversations into the search results pages, such as volume, frequency, reputation as measured by the number of followers, re-tweets, and the importance of the domain from where it has been shared. This means that you also need to have a social media strategy in order to rise to the top of your search engine results.

Of course, this aspect of Google's algorithm is subject to manipulation by automating and sending more tweets to increase the volume; however, the bottom line is that search engines are beginning to add a social layer. At the same time, there are new search engines that can monitor social conversations, the previously referred to listening tools. Thus, search and social are merging in some ways as discovery through social networks and intentional search through search engines both become important to consumers.

- ■ Facebook and Twitter are trying to improve their search capabilities (e.g., Facebook has teamed up with Microsoft on Bing™; Twitter is making it easier to search using its hashtags).
- ■ Google is providing search capabilities with a layer of social on top of its technology.

Other tools such as Topsy and socialmention are making the job of searching for and monitoring social conversations around the Web much easier.

Why is Social Discovery Becoming Important?

"Social discovery" is the new term for the way people are finding new information through their social networks. This discovery is in contrast with intentional search through a search engine. Although still useful, search engines like Google are coming up short. Many sites, which are good but young in terms of Web history, still may be hard to find since they cannot appear at the top of search rankings. In addition, peer influence and the power of serendipity are also a factor. Google requires you to be thinking about what you want, but social discovery can tell you what you might want, which then leads you to Google or another search engine to find out more.[2]

This is another testament to the power of social to elevate something new. This power works both ways as momentum for both product successes and failures. For example, Hewlett-Packard® had trouble selling its HP TouchPad due to momentum gained by bad reviews through social networks such as Twitter. A similar thing happened when Hewlett-Packard tried to get rid of its inventory at fire-sale discounts. It ran out very quickly, again through momentum picked up through social network channels.

The Power of Sharing

Today, the ease with which people can share has changed. Sharing has always occurred offline. People discovered new products, services, restaurants, and movies they met face to face. What has changed is the way in which this kind of sharing and discovering has become easy. You discover things from those with whom you have connected online, not from people you met directly. You may not know them directly, but a common association connects you, such as an online group with similar interests.

This kind of power in sharing might be a positive or a negative depending on the evaluation received. Whereas you could not easily track positive or negative word of mouth before, it is now possible to track, measure, and influence it more easily. For example, people always regarded physicians as important opinion leaders in their influence and adoption of prescription drug usage. Then, regulations allowed for direct-to-consumer advertisements in the U.S. Companies started spending millions of dollars to target consumers directly and influence them to influence their physicians. Now they had two different groups to act on their behalf to influence adoption of their products. With online tracking, companies can now find out what their prospects and customers are saying and how effective their advertisements are, based on online social conversations in forums.

Measuring Influence

You can measure influence in different ways, such as the number of discussions someone engages in about your product or the number of referrals that person makes. Another factor to consider is whether the people likely to influence – those who adopt first – do they continue to influence throughout or only when they first adopt? Do people who have recently used the product have a greater influence, or are heavy users likely to be better influencers? Research shows that network effects take time to build.[3] As a company, you have the option to use your resources in two ways:

1. You can spend all your resources sending samples and messaging to prospects; or
2. You could try to identify the most influential (or the most likely to be influential) prospects and try to influence them.

Over time, nurturing and trying to influence the influencers show greater return than continuing to send only samples or other pure marketing efforts.[4]

Social Search

Google, despite being a popular search engine, leaves a lot of room for a better search recipe. Users generally do not go beyond the first two pages of its search results and are more often left clicking on the first few results.[5] This has created a big industry in search engine optimization. Google's advice is, "Use more keywords, highlight them, and get linked on many pages." This still leaves many good finds from not being found. Google has introduced an update to its algorithm recently called Panda, which places more emphasis on quality of content.[6]

Using the example of cooking recipes, some of the food bloggers have complained about the lack of democratization in Google search results. After all, there are many specific and unique things for recipes, such as pictures, the lack or presence of ingredients, clarity of directions, or yumminess of results. A search usually results in revealing the top big ones based on "digital popularity." The problem is one of digital self-fulfilled prophecy. Since you are popular (i.e., you appear on the first page or as the first few results), you tend to get higher in your popularity rankings and, therefore, higher in the results.

Another example of Google's weakness as a search engine is the eyeglasses site that ranked high and kept getting higher,[7] despite the fact that the company was actually getting many negative reviews. Google attributed this result to its inability to take into account negative sentiments; however, this could also apply to positive digital self-prophecy.

No matter how important Google might be in getting yourself found, one can still not find many good things. While search engine optimization is important and should be an ongoing component of your strategy, until you get to the first page, you still need many other marketing tools. This is also the reason for the popularity of other social media tools, which give you the opportunity of being found and moving you up in the digital rankings.

On Facebook today, we see recommendations from friends that we come across serendipitously. Friends might also ask for personal recommendations, or for recommendations of people not known to us who are gathering online in a community of like-minded users. All of this activity points to the current weakness of search engines in their ability to accommodate four things in determining what is good enough to be at the top of the search results:

■ taste,

■ trust

■ sentiment and

■ simple refinement, which does not let the concept of "digital self-fulfilling prophecy" become dominant

Search engines are trying to make up for these weaknesses, but have ways to go. Through an announced partnership between Facebook and Bing, Microsoft will take the "likes" of people into account when presenting search results.[8] This marries the strengths of two products: Facebook has a strong social network but lacks a good search engine and Microsoft has a strong search engine but lacks a good social network. Recognizing this aspect, Google has been working to promote its own social network of Google+.[9] Even though this approach would make search results more interesting and relevant in some cases, a bias still exists since a "like" captures only positive sentiments or worse still sentiments of indeterminate value. Despite these drawbacks, the impact and recommendations of social networks on consumers is evident.

Facebook, on the other hand, still has a weakness. People do not use this site for information although it does form the backbone of sharing; the intent of users here is to interact and share. However, many social networks recognize their search deficiencies. In response, they are improving their search capabilities. Other search engines such as Topsy and socialmention are addressing this market gap by providing search results of social conversations. Twitter has its own Twitter search, which helps you find conversations based on hashtags. Currently, ordinary search and social conversation searches need different tools. This is partly the reason that Facebook and Twitter have prevented Google from gaining access to their data—partially or completely—because they recognize it as their strength.

Chapter 9 Summary and Key Takeaways

■ You cannot manually search for and monitor all the social conversations on the Web.

■ Even as Google adds a social layer to its search function, specialized tools and social search engines are stepping in to make it easier for marketers to make sense of the social conversations taking place.

■ Discovering information socially has its value to consumers in overcoming the lack of taste, trust, and serendipity associated with search engines like Google.

Chapter 10

Social Strategies:
Approaches, Integration,
and Future

By their very nature, social strategies need to be social. The focus is on building and nurturing customer relationships in order to gain permission to sell using a soft-sell approach.

Have Marketers Bought Into Social Media?

Accoriding to a report by Brian Solis on the state of social marketing, 51% of brand managers feel that social marketing will become mainstream by 2012. An equally large percentage feels that it will be at the experimental stage. Those who did not feel so positively about social marketing becoming experimental mentioned limiting reasons such as lack of budget, uncertainty about the outcomes, and lack of a social strategy. At the same time, an overwhelming majority felt that social conversations have positive outcomes such as lifting brand relevance to social consumers.[1]

One of the major benefits of nurturing and cultivating a social conversation is in building trust between customers and the company. In the book *Everywhere*,[2] Larry Weber uses the example of how Graco® managed a product recall by first going to its community and informing them, which made the recall a lot smoother for bloggers and other influential community members, helping restore parents' trust in Graco's future products. Building and nurturing a community can certainly help in such cases; however, this is no different that having your customers' general trust.

A case in point is Odwalla™ and its handling of the 1996 E. coli outbreak, which was before the era of social. Its customers already had great trust in Odwalla and were willing to forgive the company when a baby died after drinking Odwalla's unpasteurized apple juice. Odwalla handled this incident by owning up to its mistake and offering to pay for the medical expenses of affected parties. The way in which Odwalla handled this incident added to its already high trust equity.

In fact, the parent of the deceased baby said, "I don't blame the company. They did all they could."

Stephen Williamson, Chief Executive Officer, apologized publicly, offered to pay for the medical costs of those affected, set up a Website separately to communicate with the public, recalled products, communicated with employees regularly, and set up safety systems so this would not happen again.

All of these steps helped Odwalla restore the trust with its customers. Although its sales suffered in 1996, it got back on track by 1997. Social conversations can provide a boost; however, in terms of value, you must have something to work with from the beginning.[3]

Most examples of successful use of social media by companies provided by authors of current social media books are those of well known and established brands , such as Dell and Whole Foods Market—even Zappos, which is a much later entrant. One relatively lesser-known example is that of TOMS® Shoes which donates a pair of shoes to someone in need for every pair you buy. This is an example of a company whose reputation spread because of its good deeds and involvement with social causes. Whole Foods Market, on the other hand, already had a cult-like following at its stores. It has used social media to cultivate and strengthen its already tight customer relationships.

Social Strategies Need to Be Social

After search engines became popular, the industry struggled until it came up with the right advertising approach. Search engines were to find information when the customer or prospect was already thinking about a topic. Pop-ups— initially used all over the Internet, with AOL achieving notoriety—did not work simply because people were using the Internet itself to search for and find information and unrelated pop-ups were intrusive. Then, Overture Services's technology (acquired by Yahoo) introduced keyword-related ads that solved the problem of intrusive advertising making advertisements even desirable.

Today's social networks are at a similar point of intersection. Despite its huge base of 845 million users,[4] Facebook is still struggling to find the right approach to monetize its user base and get brand names to use display advertising. Many companies rightfully believe that display ads do not work and in fact interfere with users who are on social networks for other reasons.

To get around this, Facebook is now thinking along the lines of using its customers as models for its ads.[5] After all, what is more noticeable than your friends recommending products and services? However, many users might want the option not to advertise their choices.

Companies, including Facebook, are still struggling to figure out the most appropriate and rewarding social strategy. Some have benefited, such as Yelp and Zynga, which have done remarkably well socially and monetarily. The key is to figure out how to do both.

Social strategies that work best help customers do one of two things well: connect or bond.

Approaches to Social Strategies

Social strategies need to be social and strategically aligned with assets that offer a competitive advantage. People like social networks because:

- It gives them a chance to connect with people whom they do not know but who share something in common; or
- It strengthens bonds with people whom they already know in a nonintrusive, relaxing, and timesaving manner that is critical in this age of constant interruptions.

The approaches that work best are those that help customers connect or bond.[6]

This is not new. Yahoo already used this approach with its user groups. Today, the interface—especially on Facebook—and the ease with which you can share photos and videos and recommend are different. In some ways, you could say that the success of Facebook has come about because it gives you the ability to do it all in an easy-to-use interface with no walls between people.

For example, you can see what someone else, whom you do not know, has said and make a new connection. This openness, which removes privacy, also allows discovery. In addition, it combines the positives of earlier social networks, such as having the ability to communicate in a group of like-minded individuals, with the ability to recommend and read recommendations, combined with the ability to make new connections and discoveries.

For each company, it is possible to create a social network or leverage an existing one. Whether you can do that or not depends on what you have to offer. Will the community created by you benefit in a different way than what they could get elsewhere?

The desired result in a community is to bond with people of like minds. If that is not possible, your social strategy is not social. The key is to combine the success of the community with the ability to reduce costs (e.g., community members helping each other solve product issues) or increase customer acquisition and retention (e.g., community members recruiting other members because they benefit and the company stands to benefit in return).

There are two key questions for a social strategy:

1. Does it feel social to your customers, and are they making new connections or strengthening existing bonds?
2. Is it reducing cost or increasing revenues for your company?

Yelp never started out as a social network. It was merely the place to go to find out about local businesses and find the best ones based on reviews, which its customers did at no charge. Yelp depends on the free work by these reviewers to continue to be of use to its customer base. Recognizing that, Yelp has introduced recognition-based networking opportunities for those who provide the maximum number of reviews. In addition, they base this recognition on a yearly renewal cycle. Yelp pays its reviewers through recognition and nonmonetary reward.

Nurturing activity in a social network is similar to the social norms of returning a favor. For example, if a friend offers to help you, and you immediately take out your wallet, they would be offended and probably never offer to help you again. If you gave them roses, it would carry a much greater "social currency value" than the equivalent amount of dollars.

Level of Integration

According to a survey in August 2011 by The CMO Survey, companies plan to spend more on social media in the next five years up to 17.5% of their marketing budget. The same survey also showed that most companies do not integrate their social media strategies with their overall company or marketing strategy.[7] Using social media tools and creating a social media strategy involves benefiting across three important activities of a company: customers, brand, and innovation.

Although many companies have a presence known or unknown to them on many social networks such as Facebook, Twitter, and LinkedIn, only 16% say that their social media is fully integrated. For almost two-thirds, social is not in use or is in initial or pilot stages. Companies that felt they had fully integrated social media saw positive outcomes in three areas: better communication, better customer satisfaction, and better financial returns. Among the factors preventing full integration were personal, structural, and cultural. Thirty-eight percent of the respondents said that social media was high on their priority list, but the main barrier to change for the respondents was what they saw as an unclear financial return.[8]

This study brings up a couple of points:

1. The reason that many respondents do not see a positive return could be that their social media tactics are just tactics, and not a strategy tied to business objectives with a clear social media tool tracking and measuring that objective.
2. Integrating social media into marketing and corporate strategy requires a company-wide cultural shift if the culture for transparent communication and collaboration does not already exist. The fact that many report positive outcomes, such as higher customer satisfaction, could be because problems become more transparent and they can address them.

However, the structure needs to be in place within the company to address those problems. This seems to concur with some of the wisdom shared by companies already using social media. According to Robert Harles, Global Head of Social Media for Bloomberg, your social strategy should include an element of listening to customers and then tying your business objectives with insights about your customers. For example, whereas the debate between Blu-Ray and HD DVD might have lasted many years before Blu-Ray became the clear winner, today online social conversations provide a venue to figure out the result of such debates much quicker. Jen McClure, Senior Director of Social Media Strategy for Thomson Reuters, has a similar view, except she feels their organization is differentiating itself by becoming a social business. This includes training employees on the use of social media, establishing social media guidelines, getting people to understand basic principles, like "acknowledge your mistakes" or "listen to your customers."[9]

Listening to your customers is not a new principle. The concept of customer satisfaction has been around since the 1950s; however, now you can *really* listen to your customers.

*C*ustomer conversations on social media are transparent. If you do not listen, your competitor, who does, can surely benefit from it.

The blackout protest against SOPA (Stop Online Piracy Act) and PIPA (Preventing Real Online Threats to Economic Creativity and Theft of Intellectual Property Act of 2011 — the House and Senate acts to prevent piracy — is a very good example of the effective use of social media tools. Like any other effective marketing, its implementation had a creative aspect.

The blackout had the backing of big Internet heavyweights (e.g., Google, Facebook, Yahoo!, and eBay®) while the acts had the backing of equally powerful organizations such as the Recording Industry Association of America (RIAA), Motion Pictures Association of America (MPAA) and the United States Chamber of Commerce. At one point, when it seemed that the acts were likely to pass, all the social media protest gave politicians cause to pause.

The most interesting use of social media is a simple Website called blackoutsopa.org, created by Hunter Walk, Director of Product Management at YouTube, Google. The Website was very simple, providing four different badges from which to choose to use as your profile picture to protest the acts. Walk did it because he saw reports that said the debates were underreported by news networks, which were owned by corporations supporting the bills. It spread first via Twitter. As of January 18, 2012, 78,593 people had changed their profile and 8,000 had liked it on Facebook.

From this, we can conclude that social media is a powerful and unfiltered medium. It comes with a disadvantage of noise and is somewhat new. Like Middle Eastern governments, it is just a matter of time before special interest groups will also use it to tilt the debate in their favor; however, it evens the playing field and makes it more democratic. Basic requirements of creativity and imagination in marketing remain important.

The Past, the Future, and the Parallels

Unfortunately, many parallels exist between the Agricultural Age and the Information Age;[10] fortunately, we can benefit from their lessons. Nearly a century ago, farming represented the core of the U.S. workforce. Industrialization brought significant changes to farming, leading to the doubling of food production from 1820 to 1920 and doubling it even faster thereafter.[11] We had needed food for survival and now had an abundance of it.

Evolution has not kept up with the changes, and we find ourselves unable to say no. These advances have had negative effects in terms of obesity, escalating healthcare costs, environmental impact, and mass-produced cheap and unhealthy food. It has also led to a counter-revolution in agriculture in the form of organically produced, locally grown, wholesome food along with more awareness on health and food issues in the form of pressure on corporations to change. From the likes of the Tarahumara Indians, who were born to run to hunt to survive,[12] we are now at an age where we sit in front of computers, consuming information to survive.

Similar to the impact of industrialized food production, the Information Age has led to a copious amount of information—more than we can humanly handle.

Even the tools to help us manage (e.g., filters and alerts) can only go so far. Starting with the creation of language, information was always power. It helped create communities and enabled communication. We now find ourselves unable to keep up with all the information surrounding us, yet we find it difficult to tune out lest we miss something important.

Studies now show that information affects our attention span. Every time we check email and then move to a new task, it takes our brain time to readjust. Clay A. Johnson, author of

Information Diet, says that if willpower is an exhaustible resource and trainable, our attention span getting shorter and shorter is equivalent to eating fast food.[13]

Although it is admirable that McDonald's introduced an efficient fast-food industry, it has also made it impossible for people to turn away from cheap, tasty, and unhealthy food unless they draw on their willpower. In some ways, the information revolution and social media sites like Facebook are the equivalent of the efficiency of McDonald's (i.e., easy to network) and the decreased quality of information being fed to us cheaply and more liberally. It comes with its own ill effects.

*S*imilar to the counter-revolution in the food industry—with the rise of smaller, organic farms and the popularity of farmers' markets—the importance of information quality and experiences, such as face-to-face networking, is expected to take on greater significance for marketers and consumers.

In other words, *quality of created content still rules*, perhaps even more so now. Social networks have always been there, and they add a new element to your marketing portfolio through the tools they provide today.

Social Media Is a Tool, Not a Panacea

Social media is a tool for marketing to greatness on a low budget. It cannot solve all problems though. It still requires:

- Creativity and a great product or service with happy customers
- Transparency with responsiveness and a human touch
- Engagement through collaboration

You might go wrong sometimes, as the example of Sanuk Sandals in the Case Studies section later in this book shows. Television did not suddenly make every company a success. It allowed companies to express what their products could do with emotions and feelings. This is clear from McDonald's Facebook page, which shows that it has a major problem to fix with its products and its image. Having a Facebook page makes its problems transparent. Any update receives many comments from those who like as well as those who hate it. Both seem quite engaged. McDonald's has the choice to act on these responses to change its practices and perceptions.

The Future: Social Networks and the Mobile Web

Social networks, along with a mobile Web, feature very prominently today and in the future given the way consumers are using devices. As phones have become smarter and networks faster, people are turning more often to their smartphones as on-the-go information companions and to their tablets for information at home. This is especially relevant to consumer products and services, many of which we buy online or help in making in-store decisions. The two top destinations on smartphones are search and social networking sites.

The interaction between searching on smartphones and word of mouth or word of mouse seems strong (i.e., 61% stated one or the other as their motivations for search on a smartphone; they just heard about it from friends and family or from a social network they visited online).[14]

Tablets, the information companion at home, is aiding and continuing the online consumer decision journey. One in three respondents in the U.S. spends more time on their tablet than on watching television.[15] It is clear that tablets are replacing desktops and laptops as the main device for information search, reading, etc.—everything that people used to do on desktops. Although games are the top use of tablets, 56% mention using social networks on tablets.[16]

These three devices are quite interactive. Here are some facts and trends in growth to consider when moving forward:

- U.S. smartphone penetration: 47%,[17] time spent per day – 1 hour and 5 minutes,[18] continuous and on the go in short spurts[19]
- U.S. tablet penetration: 19%,[20] Time spent - 1 – 2 hours a day[21]
- U.S. television penetration: 97%,[22] Time spent 3–4 hours a day on average.[23]

In conclusion, you can see how the combination of the interaction of the tablet at home, the smartphone as the on-the-go companion, and social networks is having an impact on customer purchase behavior.

Chapter 10 Summary and Key Takeaways

■ Social strategies need to be social to be successful. This means that you provide one of two things to participants - a way to connect, or a way to bond through sharing of similar interests.

■ Successful social strategies need to combine building strong communities with cost reduction through customers helping other customers or by increasing customer retention and/or acquisition.

■ In an age of copious information, the quality of content still rules—perhaps more so than before.

■ Social media is a tool for marketing to greatness on a low budget. However, it is not a panacea. It still requires creativity, in addition to transparency, and engagement through collaboration, to succeed.

■ The interaction of the tablet at home, the smartphone on the go, and the recommendations and reviews on social networks are now dictating customer purchase behavior.

Social Success Case Studies:

How Did They Do It?

Here are four case studies of social media successes. Each has used a different strategy to engage, and each example is different - one has an established brand name, the second has no established brand name, a third is a nonprofit, and the fourth caters to businesses as opposed to end consumers.

CASE STUDY #1: NIKE (WELL-KNOWN CONSUMER BRAND)

NIKE has always used innovative approaches to selling its shoes, some of which are quite expensive. Yet, its target market, which is not affluent, will often save to buy those shoes.

NIKE initially focused on building a brand community around soccer. Its earlier forays started with efforts to build a social network with Google on top of Orkut. Since then, NIKE used MySpace to create this soccer brand community. Its largest community is on Facebook, but it has used different social networks in different countries, such as QQ in China, VKontakte in Russia, and Mxit in South Africa.[1]

NIKE created a NIKE+ community for its runners, which enables them to track their running records and health statistics, and challenge themselves and their friends. This community has 5 million members so far.[2]

NIKE has similarly expanded to creating communities around other sports categories, and can now reach 50 million people around the world through these communities.[3] The major theme is doing better in a sport and integrating the NIKE brand within that theme.

NIKE+ has over one million members in its Facebook community.[4] An update, such as one below on its Facebook community, got 715 likes and 335 comments:

"Long runs: love 'em or hate ' em? Do you listen to music, chat with friends, or get zen and enjoy the silence? Do you take breaks, or never stop moving? How do you fuel? Let us know what gets you through when you're going the distance."

The comments provide a wealth of data that NIKE could use, while keeping its members remembering the brand and engaging them at the same time. Many mentioned music; things they like to eat before, after, and during the run; what they like to drink; where they like to run; and so on. This could easily lead to the next update from NIKE, which could ask the community to tell them about the kind of music they like to listen to when running. Many NIKE+ updates have photos associated with them—ones NIKE posts or those shared by its community.

CASE STUDY #2: UNIQUE CASE STUDY OF SOCIAL MEDIA EFFECTIVENESS IN TROY, MICHIGAN (NONPROFIT)

The City of Troy, Michigan, faced the prospect of closing its library due to lack of funds, and proposed a small 0.7% tax increase.[5] This action angered some residents, resulting in a Tea Party protest against tax increases. In the loud voices raised by the well-funded Tea Party, the conversation highlighting "No taxes" soon drowned out original reason of the proposal: to save the library.

Troy used social media and a creative strategy to get attention and to put the conversation back on track. It started a campaign with a Facebook page,[6] and put posters around the neighborhood, asking people to vote "yes" to close the library and join the "bookburningparty." This enraged the townspeople, who voiced their anger on the Facebook page. It soon reached the city council, and the local, national, and even international news.

At this point, the city revealed the true intent. It released a video saying that a vote to close the library is like a vote to burn books. By now, the true nature of its campaign shifted the topic of conversations from "library" to "taxes."

On the day of the critical vote, people turned out in strong numbers to vote "yes" to save the library. The City of Troy describes its Facebook page as "A satirical effort to raise awareness and participation for a YES vote on August 2."[7] It was also an effective and low-budget campaign, using social media to change the conversation. The key is what creativity and a small budget, combined with social media tools, can achieve.

CASE STUDY #3: SANUK SANDALS (RELATIVELY UNKNOWN CONSUMER BRAND)

Most people may not have heard of Sanuk Sandals, but Deckers Outdoors recently bought the company and Sanuk achieved success through a campaign using social media tools. Its product has a cool and different feel. The designs look artistic and unlike the standard and typical sandals you see in stores.

The video on its Website focuses on the production of its advertising, a behind-the-scene look at upcoming products for Spring 2012, and a focus on the creative team rather than on the models. It has a Facebook community of 122,000 as of September 2012.[8] It also uses Instagram and Pinterest to reach its customers.

Its typical Facebook updates are as follows:

"Did you know ... Sanuks ship in biodegradable compostable corn based bags. This means not only do your feet breathe a smile-worthy sigh of relief, but

Mother Nature does too! As our friends at @hobiesurfshop say, 'Yea Earth!'"

Other updates include photographs shared by customers of various ways in which they are using their Sanuks:

Customer: *I have to say I LOVE your product but I have been waiting for nearly six weeks now, for a product that was "in-stock" when my order was placed ... so sad! :(*

Sanuk's response: *We've had some weird bugs in the system lately. And on behalf of the entire Sanuk family AND its brigade fire-breathing carrier pigeons, we apologize for the lengthy delay. Please email customercare@sanuk.com and we'll have that frown flipped upside down.*

Several themes run through Sanuk's success:

- Using a differentiated product its customers love
- Humanizing the brand
- Getting users engaged through participation
- Being responsive when the user is unhappy with comments that combine wit and concern

CASE STUDY #4 SAP COMMUNITY NETWORK (KNOWN BUSINESS BRAND)

It is more common to find B to C examples of social media successes than of B to B. This is because B to B companies tend to be more closed when it comes to engaging their business customers and partners. However, there are examples of how they have used social media successfully. One long-standing example is SAP. SAP first started by creating a community for its software developers mainly because they already collaborate and are technology savvy. Since then it has expanded to include other stakeholders such as business customers, analysts and university students.[9]

According to SAP, its community network gets 1.2 million unique visitors per month with 30,000 new members joining every month.[10] Every question gets on average 3.4 high quality responses. SAP encourages its community to participate by assigning its contributors points they can display on LinkedIn profiles.[11] It uses Facebook as well by promoting blogs of its SCN contributors.[12] Its Facebook page had about 34,000 likes as of September 2012. SAP uses Twitter mainly to promote its events before, during, and after the event.[13] For most B to B entities, internal closed networks appear to be working better although they use open networks such as Facebook, LinkedIn and Twitter as well to stay on top of the mind of its users.

Glossary and Resources

Social Media Landscape for Marketers

The world of social media has grown so much that you can now categorize it in terms of four areas: social media platforms for building communities, social media listening tools, social media management tools, and metrics.

1.   Social media platforms for building communities, of which there are many. These platforms such as Facebook and Twitter provide a place for the creation of social communities and conversations

2.   Social media listening tools help you listen to what your stakeholders are saying based on your interest. These are

somewhat similar to search engines that developed in response to the explosion of information on the Web. These tools are a response to the exponential growth of social media platforms, and the conversations on these platforms. Some are open and search based such as Topsy.

3.   Today's social media chaos for marketers has led to an explosion in the number of monitoring and management tools, which help you understand what is happening through data-based insights and easier publishing in response to what the data tell you. One example of such a tool is HootSuite for both measuring based of clicks and for managing publishing on different networks at different times. Another is SocialiQ Networks with a focus on discovery of your social surface along with a strong emphasis on security and protection of brand.

4.   Similar to the discussion of hits versus clicks at the beginning of measurement of Website performance, the explosion in social media has also led to figuring out what metrics to use in social media for performance evaluation and marketing ROI. The metrics to focus on depend on stage of the business in social media, tool used, and objectives desired.

This glossary provides a list of various players in each of these categories, and illustrates the marketing performance indicators to use at different stages of your social media journey.

Social Media Platforms – Community Building

You use social media platforms to reach your prospects and customers by publishing and engaging. All of them need to have a soft-sell approach.

Here is a list of platforms with pre-established communities and sub communities and the ability to create your own community.

Blogs (online journals): Popular ones include WordPress and Blogger

Delicious: Social network for sharing and collecting everything good you find on the Web

Facebook: Global audience with very granular information on its users; leading social network in terms of numbers and time spent online

flickr® from Yahoo!®: Site for sharing photos

Foursquare: Mobile social networking app, which allows users to check in at different locations; in return, users receive points and badges, which can be used for specials from businesses that have a presence on it (similar to Facebook Places)

FriendFeed: Real-time social sharing service, bought by Facebook; seems to serve very similar features as Facebook

Google+: An emerging but strong contender among social networks; could be important as Google ties it more to search, and as social technologies continue to merge

Instagram: App for sharing photos, which has become extremely popular; mostly important for consumer-targeted companies; Facebook bought it, but it is still retained independently

LinkedIn: Mostly professional social network, leaning towards males

Pinterest: Photo based; mostly female audience; experiencing high growth in numbers and time spent; focuses on sharing photos of hobby-related information

Reddit: Strong community to share articles. Currently has a reputation for not letting any content through that sounds like publicity initiated, trying to preserve and guard its value as a social network zealously

SlideShare: Great for sharing presentations; integrated more with LinkedIn, and caters to a professional audience

tumblr: Provides a platform for blogging along with built-in tools for publishing, sharing, and promotion

Twitter: Has a mixed audience of young and old, students and professionals, and media; great for broadcasting but with a social slant

YouTube: After Facebook, YouTube gets the maximum amount of time from social network users; important to have a presence on this for both BtoB and BtoC companies.

Social Media Listening Tools

Social media listening tools help you understand the social conversations taking place on one or more social media platforms or communities. "Listening" is the term used in the social media space. Technically, it is equivalent to "search." Google's search engine as a tool for listening to what people are saying about your brand does not perform as well as the tools below, including Google Alert.

Facebook search: Search function, though relatively not as good as Google's, still provides information on specific words, as long as they are within Facebook

Google Alerts: Set up keyword-based alerts, and get articles related to keywords delivered in your Inbox

Klout: Measures individuals' influence by assigning a score based on various social media metrics

socialmention: Search engine specializing in searching and delivering results comprised of social mentions based on a keyword; captures mentions on blogs, microblogs, and other social network conversations along with sentiment analysis at a high level

Topsy: Search engine for social conversations

Twitter search: Allows you to search for tweets based on hashtags, which is a way to identify keywords in Twitter by typing '#' in front of them

Social Media Management Tools

The proliferation of social networks, social conversations, and the increased competition to speak and be heard has resulted in social media chaos—a problem that these social media management tools have stepped in to solve. These tools help you manage your social media activities, such as making updates and viewing all the social conversations in one single dashboard. There are many and fragmented as the space itself; however, the below examples should give you an idea of the capabilities and their usage.

Awareness: Positioned as a social media marketing software, allows for publishing among different channels, managing through approvals and audits, and tracking and monitoring through reports that tell you when something was published, who published it, and the social media response

Crimson Hexagon: Positioned as a social media monitoring and analysis technology, the company uses it to go beyond sentiment analysis of social conversations

HootSuite: Competitor of TweetDeck; helps manage your updates to Twitter, Facebook, and LinkedIn

Lithium: Monitors search-specific mentions and sentiments on major social networks and outputs them in an easy-to-read report

Radian6: (now rolled into Marketing Cloud from Salesforce) Provides dashboard of insights and trends; can monitor 100+ social media sites

SocialiQ Networks: By typing in the name of your company and brands, the solution allows you to discover your brand's social accounts and owned social media presence; audit that presence for activity, application usage, and risks across social networks in order to protect them.

TweetDeck: Acquired by Twitter; application for managing tweets and updates on Facebook; allows you to search and monitor by keyword and schedule tweets

Social Media Marketing Return-on-Investment Metrics

Figuring out how to measure the return on investment in social media has been difficult. There are a number of ways to measure it, and each metric becomes important at different stages of your social media journey, depending on the business objectives for your social media efforts.

Here are some of the metrics you can use to keep track of your social media efforts in the order in which they take priority as you build your social media assets.

Social Media Metrics in Order of Priority

Likes, follows, shares, tweets (totality and growth over time): Number of people who like, follow, share, and tweet your updates or simply your social network site.

Retweets, mentions, engagement (Over time and volume): Number of times your update is retweeted, mentioned, commented on as well as percentage of your audience that does it.

Content analysis of comments (e.g., related to product quality, delivery issues, and customer service issues)

Sentiment analysis of comments Number of comments by itself does not give you as much information as the sentiment, whether what was said was positive or negative or neutral.

Share of social voice: The percentage of conversation about your company relative to your competition per social channel and across all channels in totality.

Share of social conversations around a specific problem or issue. For example, what percentage mention your brand as a solution when discussing a specific problem.

Clickthrough rates, inquiries, and leads: Did a Facebook "like" result in an inquiry or more clickthroughs on the Website?

Actual purchases: Did more tweeting result in more purchases?

Referrals after purchase: Did a purchase result in more referrals through more likes or followers?

Top 12 Messages

1. As a marketer today, you are dealing with a social Web in which your customers persuade or dissuade other customers, as opposed to a Web of sites.

2. Television did not make companies successful. Their creative strategies in using it made them successful. Social media is the same way. It is a channel. Success depends on your fundamental marketing principles.

3. Word of mouth has always been important to companies. Today, a multi-tiered form of word of mouse exists in which transparency is important, customer voice is stronger, and your marketing strategies need to be subtle and provide something of value in order to get permission to speak to your prospects and customers.

4. In a world of digital sharing, where you can track word of mouse, generating positive social conversations should be part of your company's mission.

5. Each social network has different demographics and usage patterns. Your focus and choice of social networks should depend on where your target market spends its time.

6. Marketers have always coveted publicity as an earned media. Today, earned media has taken on more importance due to fragmentation of channels and an empowered customer voice.

7. What social media conversations can teach you can be revealing about lack of processes, checks, and priorities in place internally.

8. Before you start using social media tools, have a solid foundation in products and processes; otherwise, be prepared to hear what you fear and take the steps to fix it.

9. Proliferation in social media content has resulted in a proliferation of quantity over quality, or rather the inability to separate quality from quantity in the noise despite all of the available search tools.

10.   Sentiment analysis in social media only captures the feelings of the most passionate. To make better sense of it, use benchmarking to gauge the volume and trends in the volume of positive and negative sentiments.

11.   Social strategies that work best are the ones that help customers do one of two things well: connect or bond.

12.   Similar to the counter-revolution in the food industry—with the rise of smaller, organic farms and the popularity of farmer's markets—the importance of quality of information and experiences, such as face-to-face networking, will take on greater significance for marketers and consumers.

About the Author

Sujata Ramnarayan, Ph.D., a former Gartner Group Senior Analyst and a former Assistant Professor of Marketing at Humboldt State University (a California State University), currently provides Research, Advisory, Speaking, and Training Services through her company SMStrat (http://www.smstrat.com), conducting research at the cusp of marketing, technology, and customer behavior.

Dr. Ramnarayan currently also serves as a board member of CareerCloset, a non-profit, as a Strategic Marketing Advisor and as the VP of Digital Marketing for the Silicon Valley American Marketing Association. Her most recent articles have been published by MarketingProfs.com and the Marketing Management Magazine. Ms. Ramnarayan holds a BS. In Math, an M.B.A, and a Ph.D in Marketing. You may reach her @mktgnugget or at info@smstrat.com.

Endnotes

Purpose of this Book

[1] "The State of Social Media Marketing," *Survey by Awareness Inc*, September 2012.

Chapter 1: Social Networks and the Empowered Customer

[1] "How Martin Luther Went Viral," *The Economist*, December 17–30, 2011.

[2] "How Discovery Will Drive Transactions," *TechCrunch*, Aug. 21, 2011, http://techcrunch.com/2011/08/21/how-discovery-will-drive-transactions

[3] "The Untold Story of How the Internet Forced Bill Gates to Reverse Course," *Business Week*, July 15, 1996.

Chapter 2: The Dawn of Social Networks

[1] "Why Americans Use Social Media," *PewInternet.org*, November 15, 2011, http://www.pewinternet.org/Reports/2011/Why-Americans-Use-Social-Media.aspx

[2] "Social Networking Sites and Our Lives," *PewInternet.org*, June 16, 2011, http://pewinternet.org/Reports/2011/Technology-and-social-networks.aspx

[3] "It's a Social World: Top 10 Need-to-Knows About Social Networking and Where It's Headed," *ComScore Whitepaper*, December 21, 2011.

[4] Matt Carmichael, "The Demographics of Social Media," *Ad Age Blogs*, May 16, 2011, http://adage.com/article/adagestat/demographics-facebook-linkedin-myspace-twitter/227569

[5] Ibid Note 4.

[6] "Study: Social Networking Sites Overtake Porn as Internet's #1 Search," *Huffington Post*, September, 20008, http://www.huffingtonpost.com/2008/09/17/study-social-networking-s_n_127122.html.

[7] "State of the Media: The Social Media Report," *Nielsen.com*, Q3 2011, http://cn.nielsen.com/documents/Nielsen-Social-Media-Report_FINAL_090911.pdf

[8] "Facebook, LinkedIn, and Twitter User Demographics and Behavior: Who are they and how engaged are they?" *SMStrat*, September 2011.

[9] "Twitter Use 2012," *PewInternet.org*, May 31, 2012 ,http://pewinternet.org/Reports/2012/Twitter-Use-2012.aspx.

[10] Supra, Note 7

[11] "Social Demographics: Who's Using Today's Biggest Networks," *Mashable.com*, March 9, 2012 ,http://mashable.com/2012/03/09/social-media-demographics/

[12] Ibid Note 8.

[13] Supra, Note 7.

[14] "The Mounting Minuses at Google+," *The Wall Street Journal*, February 28, 2012.

[15] Ibid Note 13.

[16] Timothy Egan, "Please Stop Sharing," *The New York Times*, December 15, 2011 http://opinionator.blogs.nytimes.com/2011/12/15/please-stop-sharing/?hp

[17] Larry Weber, *Everywhere—Comprehensive Digital Business Strategy for a Social Media Era*, John Wiley and Sons, 2011.

[18] "Meh! Not Everyone's Into Social Networks," *MarketingProfs.com*, http://www.mpdailyfix.com/meh-not-everyones-into-social-networks/

[19] Ibid Note 17.

[20] "Form S1 Registration by Facebook," February 12, 2012, *Securities and Exchange Commission.*

[21] "Putting Facebook to Work For Business," *AMA Webcast*, December 13, 2011. Presented by Brian Brinkmann, Senior Director, Product Marketing, MicroStrategy.

Chapter 3: Building a Social Media Strategy

[1] "Social Media Spend Continues To Soar," *CMOsurvey.org* http://cmosurvey.org/blog/social-media-spend-continues-to-soar.

[2] Ron Safko, *The Social Media Bible*, Second Edition, John Wiley and Sons, 2010.

[3] "Pebble: E-Paper Watch for iPhone and Android," April 12, 2012, http://www.kickstarter.com/projects/597507018/pebble-e-paper-watch-for-iphone-and-android/posts/206882

[4] "Pebble Technology Becomes Kickstarter Test Case," *The Wall Street Journal*, July 2, 2012.

[5] "Leveraging the Talent Driven Organization," *The Aspen Institute*, 2010.

[6] "Social Networking Sites and Our Lives," *PewInternet.org*, June 2011.

[7] "Linkedin's 'Share' Button: Here's The Secret Behind Its Disproportionate Power In Social Media," *Business Insider*, http://www.businessinsider.com/linkedins-share-button-the-secret-behind-disproportional-power-2011-12

Chapter 4: Word of Mouse

[1] Emanuel Rosen, *The anatomy of buzz*, Double Day, 2000.

[2] Ibid Note 1.

[3] Jerry Wilson, *Word of Mouth Marketing*, John Wiley and Sons, 1991.

[4] "Firms Take Online Reviews to Heart," *The Wall Street Journal*, July 29, 2012.

[5] V. Kumar, et al., "How Valuable is Word of Mouth?" *Harvard Business Review*, October 2007.

[6] Supra, Note 1.

[7] Supra, Note 3.

[8] Andy Sernovitz, *Word of Mouth Marketing: How Smart Companies get People Talking*, Kaplan Publishing, 2006.

[9] Ed Keller and Brad Fay, *The Face-to-Face Book*, Free Press, 2012.

[10] "Too Much Buzz," *The Economist*, December 31, 2011.

[11] "What Makes a Great Tweet," *Harvard Business Review*, May 2012.

[12] "How Consumers Interact with Brands on Facebook," *Mashable.com*, September 12, 2011, http://mashable.com/2011/09/12/consumers-interact-facebook/

[13] Supra, Note 5.

[14] Everett Rogers, *Diffusion of Innovations*, Free Press, 2003.

[15] Kozinets, Robert V., et al., "Networked narratives, understanding word of mouth marketing in online communities," *Journal of Marketing*, Volume 74, March 2010.

[16] Ibid Note15.

[17] "Same Game New Rules," *Marketing Management*, Winter 2011, pp. 4-9.

[18] "#fail: Hashtag Revolts Show Marketing Doesn't Work on Social Media," *Time Magazine*, January 26, 2012 http://techland.time.com/2012/01/26/hashtag-revolts-show-marketing-doesnt-work-on-social-media/

[19] Ibid Note 18.

[20] "McDonald's Immediately Follows Its Epic #McDStories Fail With Another Twitter Campaign," *Business Insider* http://www.businessinsider.com/mcdonalds-is-following-its-epic-mcdstories-fail-with-another-twitter-hashtag-campaign-2012-1

Chapter 5: Role of the Community in Social Networks

[1] "Who Knows?," *The Guardian*, October 25, 2004 http://www.guardian.co.uk/technology/2004/oct/26/g2.onlinesupplement

[2] Ibid Note 1

[3] Supra, Note 1.

[4] "The Cathedral and the Bazaar," Eric Steven Raymond, 2000, http://catb.org/~esr/writings/homesteading/cathedral-bazaar/

[5] Ibid Note 4. (Emphasis added)

[6] Supra Note 4.

[7] Windows is a registered trademark of Microsoft Corporation in the United States and other countries.

[8] "Why Yelp Works," *The New York Times*, May 12, 2008, http://bits.blogs.nytimes.com/2008/05/12/why-yelp-works/

[9] "Yelp's Online Reviewing Mafia," *BloombergBusinessweek Magazine*, June 2, 2011, http://www.businessweek.com/magazine/content/11_24/b4232083260194.htm.

[10] Ibid Note 9.

[11] Comment online from CEO Jeremy Stoppelson in response to "Why Yelp Works," *New York Times*, May 12, 2008, http://bits.blogs.nytimes.com/2008/05/12/why-yelp-works/#comment-198253.

12 "The Woman Behind Angie's List," *Inc.com*
,http://www.inc.com/magazine/20100501/the-woman-behind-angies-list.html.

13 "No Free Stuff Here: At Angie's List, Members Pay," *The Wall Street Journal*, October 6, 2010
,http://online.wsj.com/article/SB10001424052748703843804575534493983291732.html.

14 "Angie's List? It's Not What You Think It Is …," *Papoom.com*,
http://www.papoom.com/AngiesListReview-01.htm.

15 Susan Fournier and Sara Lee, "Getting brand communities right," *Harvard Business Review*, April 2009.

16 "Giving it All Away," *metroactive*, May 1997,
http://www.metroactive.com/papers/metro/05.08.97/cover/linus-9719.html.

17 Supra, Note 15.

18 "How to Use Gamification to Build Digital Loyalty," *smstrat.com*,
http://smstrat.com/2012/08/how-to-use-gamification-to-build-digital-loyalty/.

Chapter 6: Trust and Taste

1 "Trust Modeling and Management: from Social Trust to Digital Trust," Book Chapter of *Computer Security, Privacy, and Politics: Current Issues, Challenges, and Solutions*, IGI Global, 2007.

2 "Got Twitter? You Have Been Scored," *The New York Times*, June 25, 2011, http://www.nytimes.com/2011/06/26/sunday-review/26rosenbloom.html?_r=1.

3 "The Significance of Reputation and Brand for Creating Trust in the Different Stages of a Relationship between an Online Vendor and it Customers," Sabine Einwiller, *Eighth Research Symposium on Emerging Electronic Markets*, 2001.

[4] Sabine Einwiller, "The significance of reputation and brand for creating trust in the different stages of a relationship between an online vendor and its customers," *Eighth Research Symposium on Emerging Electronic Markets*, 2001.

[5] Sally Bibb and Jeremy Kourdy, *A Question of Trust*, PALGRAVE MACMILLAN, 2004.

[6] "Same game, new rules: Unilever's former CEO discusses the future of brand marketing," *Marketing Management*, Winter 2011, p. 4.

[7] "With new laws, traffic take a backseat," *The Wall Street Journal*, January 19, 2012.

[8] Supra, Note 17, Chapter 4.

[9] "Edward Bernays, " *Wikipedia*, http://en.wikipedia.org/wiki/Edward_Bernays.

[10] "Should You Trust Online Reviews," *Slate.com*, August 2012, http://www.slate.com/articles/business/the_dismal_science/2012/08/tripadvisor_expedia_yelp_amazon_are_online_reviews_trustworthy_economists_weigh_in_.single.html,

[11] Supra, Note 5.

[12] Supra, Note 5.

[13] Supra, Note 5.

[14] "Building Trust in Business 2012: How Top Companies Leverage Trust, Leadership, and Collaboration," *The Human Capital Institute*, June 2012, http://www.hci.org/about/press-releases/building-trust-business-2012-how-top-companies-leverage-trust-leadership-and

[15] Shani Higgins, CEO, Technorati, Speaking at a Direct Marketing Association Event, 2012 (*with permission to quote*).

[16] Ricardo Semler, *Maverick: The Success Story Behind the World's Most Unusual Workplace*, Warner Books, 1993.

[17] Adam Lashinsky, *Inside Apple: How America's Most Admired—and Secretive—Company Really Works*, John Murray, 2012.

[18] Jim Collins, *Good to Great,* HarperCollins Publishers Inc., 2001.

[19] Supra, Note 5.

[20] "P&G's Marketing Chief Looks to go Digital," *The Wall Street Journal,* March 15, 2012.

[21] "Death of the Salesman," *The Wall Street Journal,* March 15, 2012.

[22] "Glenn Beck Rallies Troops for Revolution Against TV," *The Wall Street Journal,* March 15, 2012.

[23] "Reviews, Reputation, and Revenue: The Case of Yelp.com," Working Paper by Michael Luca, *Harvard Business School,* September 2011.

[24] "Should You Trust Online Reviews," *Slate.com,* August 2012, http://www.slate.com/articles/business/the_dismal_science/2012/08/tripadvisor_expedia_yelp_amazon_are_online_reviews_trustworthy_economists_weigh_in_.single.html.

[25] "A Bully Finds a Pulpit on the Web," *New York Times,* November 26, 2010, http://www.nytimes.com/2010/11/28/business/28borker.html?pagewanted=all.

[26] "Google Changes its Rank Algorithm in Response to DecorMyEyes Story," *TechCrunch,* December 2010, http://techcrunch.com/2010/12/01/googl/.

[27] "When You Shouldn't Listen To Your Critics," *Harvard Business Review,* June 2011.

Chapter 7: Return on Investment

[1] "Introducing 'Go Social,'" *PCWorld,* January 26, 2012 http://www.pcworld.com/businesscenter/article/248680/introducing_go_social.html.

[2] "Does Social Media Have a Return on Investment," *FastCompany,* June 2011, http://www.fastcompany.com/1760849/does-social-media-have-return-investment.

[3] Ibid Note 2.

[4] "How Much Is a Facebook Fan Worth? $10. Or Possibly 2 Cents." *WebGuild*, November 22, 2011, http://www.Webguild.org/20111122/how-much-is-a-facebook-fan-worth-10-or-possibly-2-cents.

[5] "Why Brands Still Need Facebook 'Fans,'" *AdAge*, November 22, 2011, http://adage.com/article/digital/study-facebook-fan-worth-10-average-brands/231128/.

[6] "Average Value of Facebook Fan: $136.38," *MarketingProfs .com*, http://www.marketingprofs.com/charts/2010/3713/average-value-of-facebook-fan-13638.

[7] Supra, Note 5.

[8] "Linkedin's 'Share' Button: Here's The Secret Behind Its Disproportionate Power In Social Media, " *Business Insider* http://www.businessinsider.com/linkedins-share-button-the-secret-behind-disproportional-power-2011-12.

[9] "Video: Facebook Defends Ads After Criticism," *The Wall Street Journal*, June 2012, http://live.wsj.com/video/facebook-defends-ads-after-criticism-/F5C390D1-741D-43AE-930C-120A84C1D130.html?KEYWORDS=facebook+AND+advertising+effectiveness#!F5C390D1-741D-43AE-930C-120A84C1D130

[10] "Why Social Media is Not Free," *Marketing Management Magazine*, Summer 2012, p. 18.

[11] Oliver Blanchard, *Social Media ROI*, Pearson Education, 2011.

[12] Supra, Note 8 ,Chapter 2.

[13] Supra Note 11.

[14] Sally Bibb and Jeremy Kourdy, *A Question of Trust*, Marshall Cavendish Limited, 2007.

[15] "The Man Behind Facebook's Marketing," *The Wall Street Journal*, February 2, 2012.

[16] "Facebook Shrinks Six Degrees of Separation to Just 4.74," *Huffington Post*, November 2011, http://www.huffingtonpost.com/2011/11/22/facebook-six-degrees-separation_n_1107577.html.

[17] "The Button That Made Facebook Billions," *The Wall Street Journal*, February 2, 2012.

[18] "P&G's Marketing Chief Looks to Go Digital," *The Wall Street Journal*, March 14, 2012.

[19] Shaomei et al., "Who Says What To Whom on Twitter," *WWW 2011*, March 28-April 1, 2011.

[20] Ibid Note 19.

[21] Supra Note 19.

[22] Supra Note 19.

[23] "State of Social Marketing," Annual Survey Report (2012), sponsored by Awareness Social Marketing Software.

[24] "NYU Researchers Discover Social Media Impact on Retailers" http://www.crimsonhexagon.com/customers/nyu-social-media-study/.

[25] "I'd Like to Thank My Twitter Followers," *The Wall Street Journal*, February 24, 2012 http://online.wsj.com/article/SB10001424052970203358704577237242516804580.html

[26] "First Look: Survey Warns Of Consumers Turning Off From Digital Ads," *TechCrunch* http://techcrunch.com/2012/02/24/first-look-survey-warns-of-consumers-turning-off-from-digital-ads/

[27] "What Marketers Can Learn from Wholefoods's Organic Approach to Pinterest," *Mashable.com*, February 23, 2012.

[28] Ibid, Note 27.

[29] Supra, Note 27.

[30] "Interactive Marketing Spend Will Near $77 Billion By 2016," *Forbes*, August 25, 2011,

http://www.forbes.com/sites/forrester/2011/08/25/interactive-marketing-spend-will-near-77-billion-by-2016/.

[31] "Trends in Consumers' Time Spent With Media," *eMarketer*, December 28, 2010, http://www.emarketer.com/%28S%28eqpd0445sqvknv45k1apd345%29%29/Article.aspx?R=1008138.

[32] "Q3 '11 Internet Advertising Revenues Up 22% from Year Ago, Climb to Nearly $7.9 Billion, According to IAB and PwC," *Interactive Advertising Bureau (IAB)*, http://www.iab.net/about_the_iab/recent_press_releases/press_release_archive/press_release/pr-113011.

[33] "US Online Advertising Spending to Surpass Print in 2012, *"eMarketer*, January 19, 2012 http://www.emarketer.com/PressRelease.aspx?R=1008788.

[34] Ibid Note 33.

[35] "TV's Big Ad-Sales Bazaar Inspires an Online Copycat," *The Wall Street Journal*, February 17, 2012.

[36] Supra, Note 30.

[37] "American Time Use Survey Summary," *Bureau of Labor Statistics*, June 2012, http://www.bls.gov/news.release/atus.nr0.htm.

[38] "10.5 Billion Minutes Spent on Facebook Daily, Excluding Mobile," *ZDnet*, March 2012, http://www.zdnet.com/blog/facebook/10-5-billion-minutes-spent-on-facebook-daily-excluding-mobile/11034.

[39] "Interactive Marketing Spend Will Near $77 Billion by 2016," *Forrester*, August 24, 2011, http://blogs.forrester.com/shar_vanboskirk/11-08-24-interactive_marketing_spend_will_near_77_billion_by_2016.

[40] "TV Ad Spending Largely Unaffected by Growth Online," *eMarketer.com*, March 2011, http://www.emarketer.com/Article.aspx?R=1008304.

[41] "Kantar Media Reports U.S. Advertising Expenditures Increased 0.8% in 2011," *KanterMedia.com*, March 2012, http://www.kantarmedia.com/sites/default/files/press/Kantar_Media_2011_Q4_US_Ad_Spend.pdf.

42 "P & G's Marketing Chief Looks To Go Digital," *The Wall Street Journal*, March 13, 2012.

43 Vivek Subramanian, Co-Founder and VP of Products, CalmSea Inc. (*Quoted with permission*)

44 Ibid Note 43.

45 "Newspapers Lose $10 in Print for Every Digital $1," *Business Week*, March 19, 2012.

46 "Nearly Half of American Adults Are Smartphone Owners," *Pewresearch.org*, March 1, 2012 http://pewresearch.org/pubs/2206/smartphones-cell-phones-blackberry-android-iphone.

47 "E-book Sales Surge After Holidays," *USA Today*, January 9, 2012, http://www.usatoday.com/life/books/news/story/2012-01-09/ebooks-sales-surge/52458672/1.

Chapter 8: Role of Websites in a Social Web

1 "Startups Resist Facebook's Pull," *The Wall Street Journal*, March 14, 2012.

Chapter 9: Role of Search Engines in a Social Web

1 "Google Launches Search Plus Your World," *Search Engine Watch*, January 20, 2012, http://searchenginewatch.com/article/2136615/Google-Launches-Search-Plus-Your-World.

2 "How Discovery Will Drive Transactions," *TechCrunch*, August 21, 2011, http://techcrunch.com/2011/08/21/how-discovery-will-drive-transactions.

3 "Opinion Leadership and Social Contagion in New Product Diffusion," *Marketing Science*, March-April 2011, Vol 30, No2.

4 Ibid Note 3.

[5] "2nd Page Rankings: Youre The # 1 Loser," *Gravitateonline.com*, April 2011, http://www.gravitateonline.com/google-search/2nd-place-1st-place-loser-seriously.

[6] "Facts About Google and Competition." http://www.google.com/competition/howgooglesearchworks.html.

[7] "A Bully Finds a Pulpit on the Web," *The New York Times*, November 26, 2010, http://www.nytimes.com/2010/11/28/business/28borker.html?pagewanted=all.

[8] "Facebook and Bing's Plan to Make Search Social," *Mashable Social Media*, October 13, 2010 http://mashable.com/2010/10/13/facebook-bing-social-search.

[9] "Critics Accuse Google of Unfairly Promoting Google+ in Search Results," *PCWorld*, January 11, 2012, http://www.pcworld.com/article/247908/critics_accuse_google_of_unfairly_promoting_google_in_search_results.html.

Chapter 10: Social Strategies: Approaches, Integration, and Future

[1] Brian Solis, "The State of Social Marketing 2012," December 6, 2011, http://www.briansolis.com/2011/12/the-state-of-social-marketing-2011-2012.

[2] Larry Weber, *Everywhere: Comprehensive Digital Business Strategy for the Social Media Era*, John Wiley & Sons, 2011.

[3] "Companies in Crisis—What To Do When It All Goes Wrong," *Mallen Baker* , http://www.mallenbaker.net/csr/crisis05.html.

[4] Form S-1 Registration Statement, Facebook Inc., February 2012, *Securities and Exchange Commission*.

5 "Facebook's New Advertising Model: You," *Forbes*, November 16, 2011, http://www.forbes.com/sites/roberthof/2011/11/16/facebooks-new-advertising-model-you/2/.

6 Mikotaj jan Piskorski, "Social Strategies That Work," *Harvard Business Review*, November 2011.

7 "Integrating Social Media," *Marketing Management*, Winter 2011, pp. 16–17.

8 "Integrating Social Media Still Challenges Marketers," *MarketingProfs.com* http://www.marketingprofs.com/charts/2012/6855/integrating-social-media-still-challenges-marketers10.

9 "Social Media: 3 Steps From 3 Great Companies," *Forbes*, September 15, 2011 http://www.forbes.com/sites/sap/2011/09/15/social-media-3-steps-from-3-great-companies/.

10 Clay A. Johnson, The Information Diet: A Case for Conscious Consumption, O'Reilly Media, Inc., 2012.

11 Ibid Note 11.

12 Christopher McDougall, Born to Run: A Hidden Tribe, Superathletes, and the Greatest Race the World Has Never Seen, Random House Inc., 2009.

13 Supra, Note 10.

14 "The Mobile Movement: Understanding Smartphone Users," *Google Study*, April, 2011.

15 "Understanding Tablet Device Users," *Google/AdMob Study*, March 2011.

16 Ibid Note 16.

17 "ComScore: U.S. Smartphone Penetration 47% in Q2; Android Remains Most Popular, But Apple's Growing Faster," *TechCrunch*, August 2012, http://techcrunch.com/2012/08/01/comscore-us-smartphone-penetration-47-in-q2-android-remains-most-popular-but-apples-growing-faster/.

18 "TV, Mobile See Gains in Viewing Time," *eMarketer*, December 2011, http://www.emarketer.com/Article.aspx?R=1008728.

[19] "Americans and Their Cellphones," August 2011, *PewInternet.org*, http://pewinternet.org/Reports/2011/Cell-Phones.aspx.

[20] "Tablet and E-book Reader Ownership Nearly Double Over the Holiday Gift-Giving Period," January 2012, *PewInternet.org*, http://cms.pewresearch.org/pewinternet/files/2012/03/Pew_Tablets-and-e-readers-double-1.23.2012.pdf.

[21] "Survey Claims Tablets Used Primarily For Gaming," *TGDaily.com*, April 2011, http://www.tgdaily.com/business-and-law-features/55303-google-survey-finds-tablets-used-primarily-for-gaming.

[22] "Nielsen Estimates Number of US Television Homes to be 114.7 Million," March 2011, *Nielsen.com*, http://blog.nielsen.com/nielsenwire/media_entertainment/nielsen-estimates-number-of-u-s-television-homes-to-be-114-7-million/.

[23] Ibid Note 19.

Social Success Case Studies: How Did They Do It?

[1] "How Nike Outruns the Social Media Competition," *Mashable.com*, September 22, 2011, http://mashable.com/2011/09/22/nike-social-media/.

[2] Ibid Note 1.

[3] Ibid Note 1.

[4] http://www.facebook.com/Nikerunning.

[5] "Leo Burnett Detroit Stages a Book Burning Party," *The Denver Egotist*, March 25, 2012, http://www.thedenveregotist.com/news/national/2012/march/25/leo-burnett-detroit-stages-book-burning-party.

[6] Ibid Note 5.

[7] http://www.facebook.com/BookBurningParty

[8] http://www.facebook.com/SanukFootwear?ref=ts

---

[9] "Leveraging the Talent Driven Organization," *The Aspen Institute,* 2010.

[10] SAP, http://scn.sap.com/docs/DOC-18503

[11] Supra, Note 9.

[12] http://www.facebook.com/sapcommunitynetwork

[13] Supra, Note 9.